The Emotional Side of Money

The Emotional Side of Money

a roadmap to financial wellness

TARI K. VICKERY

SHE WRITES PRESS

Published in 2026 by
She Writes Press, an imprint of The Stable Book Group

1569 Solano Ave #546
Berkeley, CA 94707
https://shewritespress.com
The Library of Congress Control Number is available upon request.
ISBN: 979-8-89636-300-2
eISBN: 979-8-89636-301-9

Interior Designer: Tabitha Lahr

Printed in the United States

Names and identifying characteristics have been changed to protect the privacy of certain individuals.

For Grandma and Meme, whose love nurtured me,
and for Kent, Heather, Charles, and Amina,
whose love sustains me.

CONTENTS

Introduction ix

PART I: WHERE WE FIND OURSELVES

Chapter 1: How Did We Get Here? 3
Chapter 2: How to Shift Your Thinking 15
Chapter 3: Let's Talk About Money 21
Chapter 4: How to Talk with Others 37

PART II: HOW WE THINK ABOUT MONEY

Chapter 5: When Financial Stress Feels Overwhelming 45
Chapter 6: Personal Identity Around Money 61
Chapter 7: How We Make Financial Decisions 75
Chapter 8: Gender Income Inequality 99
Chapter 9: Ways We Earn Money 113
Chapter 10: Needs vs. Wants 127
Chapter 11: How Much Is Enough? 139
Chapter 12: Why Not a Budget? 151
Chapter 13: When Our Financial World Turns Upside Down 163

PART III: MONEY WITHIN FAMILIES

Chapter 14: Partners and Money 173
Chapter 15: Kids and Money 191
Chapter 16: Families and Money 211
Chapter 17: Dying and Money 231

PART IV: GOING FORWARD

Chapter 18: A Testimony: My Journey to Financial Wellness 247
Chapter 19: Your Journey to Financial Wellness 251

Notes 255
Acknowledgments 261
About the Author 263

Introduction

Let's face it . . . Talking or even thinking about money can be scary, difficult, and excruciatingly painful. Furthermore, discussing it with others is often considered taboo in "polite society." Many of us have been taught that it is rude to discuss money with others. We've gotten some loud and clear messages—with little or no guidance, training, or resources to help us learn how to think about or manage money:

Don't talk, don't trust, don't feel,
don't ask questions. Oh, and by the way . . .
make good decisions that will ensure a
lifetime of financial security.

Therefore, we have little or no roadmap for how to process experiences from our childhood related to money or how to make sense of events that happened with our parents (including those for which it's unlikely any sense could ever be made). We suffer in silence, without any idea why money triggers us in ways we rarely explore. We're unaware that our emotions, and possibly experiences, are similar to those our friends and partners have endured. We don't know how to talk about money with a trusted friend, or where to get guidance as to how we might talk about it, or with whom.

As we take this journey together, you'll begin to have a new appreciation for some of the sources of your frustration. You will understand why you struggle with your awareness of what you think about money or how to manage it. You will learn how unresolved money trauma, emotional spending, and inherited beliefs can control your financial reality—often more than income or education ever could. In the process, you'll manage your money better because you'll be in control of it, instead of allowing emotions to drive your decisions.

I should warn you that you're about to embark on a roller coaster ride of emotions as we travel down this road. You might ask why anyone would intentionally stir up emotions of angst, conflict, dread, and perhaps trauma. I'd guess that you are willing to do it to stop the heart-pounding you feel when you think about money. After all, you've bought the book and read this far.

Before we go any further, let me add that I've heard this question from many clients and friends through the years: "What's wrong with me? Other people manage their money. I don't know why this is so hard." To which I reply: *"There's nothing wrong with you!"*

You haven't been taught the skills you need to manage your money or have a constructive relationship with it. The same mind that helps you function well in other aspects of everyday living gets its wires crossed when the topic is money, making you feel like your brain has been hijacked. You have likely been confused, wounded, or traumatized around money. Together, we'll sort through issues that will help you improve your relationship with your money.

Keep in mind that rare is the home where money is discussed in a way that enhances our financial literacy. Few people are comfortable discussing the topic. Parents often find it difficult to guide their children on how to think about money or manage their finances. Money and sex seem to be secret subjects for many parents, ones they think their kids will figure out when the time is right, like they did themselves (or perhaps didn't). We'll leave the sex discussion for others to contemplate, but in many American homes, money comes up for discussion only during disagreements about how it is used, sometimes accompanied by fear, anger, dread, and feelings of deprivation. This dysfunctional relationship with money often continues into the next generation.

A word of caution: You might find yourself feeling negative emotions toward your parents as we cover some topics. I encourage you to remember with compassion that our parents were doing their best during a different era, likely continuing patterns they learned from their parents. I've never known a parent who intentionally set out to make their kid's life more difficult than it needed to be.

You'll find that this endeavor to know yourself in the context of money doesn't follow a straight line. Influenced by family history, it's more like a mountain range with sharp peaks, surprising drop-offs, and the occasional beautiful view. As memories will most likely stir up strong emotions, I encourage you to be gentle with yourself as you unpack a lifetime of observations and experiences. It is my hope that our time together will provide a catalyst for you to explore the genesis of your thoughts about money, perhaps for the first time in your life. This journey will help you better understand why some of your choices and habits don't serve you well.

A bit of my personal history might be helpful to understand how my early views on money were shaped. I grew up with deeply rooted fears around money as the second child of a single mother who was just nineteen when I was born. I'll tell you details later, but by the time I was a preteen, I'd spent several years as a child and grandchild of family business owners, which provided a wealth of opportunities to internalize how money impacts nearly every aspect of daily life.

I'll tell you how owning a business with my husband for ten years early in our marriage ended in losing our income, retirement savings, home, and lifestyle. How that business failure became a gift as it resulted in our family's move to Palo Alto, California, when I was forty, so I could earn my undergraduate and master's degrees in sociology from Stanford University. How my sociological training and business experience intertwined, allowing me to help high-tech startup entrepreneurs form and grow their fledgling businesses. And how the combination of my academic training along with business and life experiences has guided my current work of more than twenty-five years as the owner of Life Matters Financial Group. In my work, I've been privileged to be intimately involved with clients' thoughts, decisions, habits, explorations, successes, struggles, and trauma around money.

Sociology taught me how family dynamics, societal implications, marketing, advertising, and myriad other factors impact our daily financial decisions. We don't spend money in a vacuum. This knowledge and business experience have allowed me to build and enjoy long-lasting relationships with dozens of clients and several multigenerational families around their money. While the specifics of our work together vary with each client, the core focus remains the same: helping clients understand their financial patterns and ways their ideas around money can negate otherwise rational thinking.

From their stories and case histories, you will see that you're not alone. You will get the added benefit of seeing how things worked out for others, whether positively or negatively. We'll look at their stories to see where and how you have similar experiences, noticing what triggers your emotions so that you can better understand your relationship with money. My hope is that this book will provide a framework that helps you clarify your own ideas around money. Then, you can decide which of your strategies to continue to use or change in your effort to gain and maintain control of your finances and make peace with them.

Keep in mind that many factors play a part in the ways we think about money and the choices we make. In the chapters that follow, we'll see how the following issues can affect our general thinking about money and choices about how we spend it:

- family dynamics and opinions about spending, saving, and investing money
- geographical location
- sources of income
- identifying items as "needs" or "wants"
- gender differences and inequalities
- factors we consider when making financial decisions
- ideas about what constitutes wealth and financial security
- consequences that result from abundance and scarcity thinking

As we explore together, I will share details of my own journey around money, as well as my experiences working with individuals and families around theirs. I'll introduce you to my immediate family: Kent, my husband of fifty years; our Gen X and millennial children, Heather and Charles, who are ten years apart in age; and our teenage granddaughter, Amina. Along our journey to explore beliefs about money and enhance your relationship with yours, you'll also meet some of my friends, clients, and colleagues.

While it's often helpful to talk through our ideas with someone else, I encourage you to first explore your reactions and thoughts about money either individually or with your therapist, before discussing them with your partner, trusted friend, or immediate family member. Because the topic of money is fraught with triggers and emotions, it's helpful to be aware of what's happening inside you before engaging with someone else who likely has their own issues around money. I'll include questions at the end of each chapter to help guide your thoughts and potential conversations.

If you like to physically engage with your learning environment, you might start by writing a letter to your money to describe your anxieties, better understand your feelings about it, and identify specific ways you'd like to change your personal relationship with it. You might remind it of your past and current relationship, telling it your hopes for your future together. For example, your letter might start:

> *Dear Money,*
> *You make my heart race. You sabotage my happiness. I'd like to better understand why you have this effect on me.*

> Or, perhaps: *I would like more of you.*

> And it might close: *I am working on improving my relationship with you. Please be patient.*

After you finish reading this book, you might write a second letter to it and compare the two letters to see how your relationship has changed as a result of this journey we've taken together.

Please keep in mind that my insights, observations, and experiences are revealed through my lens as an American, Caucasian, upper-middle-class, third-aged woman who is inherently biased by the circumstances of my birth and experiences of my specific life. I was raised in Oklahoma, where I spent most of my first forty years. I lived more than two decades in California before spending recent years living my best life on the Hawaiian island of Kaua'i.

Before we begin, let's also remember that discussions around money require a level of confidentiality second to none. I've shared my own stories to the best of my recollection and have been given permission to share specific stories from friends, colleagues, and clients. I've chosen to mask identifying information, other than that of my family. I've shared memories of both my family and others to describe concepts, actions, and outcomes. I've also taken the liberty of creating composite stories of clients and friends when it would illuminate a particular concept. Storytelling is an art, one that is meant to engage you to explore, while providing information to help you see yourself in the stories of others that will elicit memories of your own experiences.

Let's begin!

SOMETHING TO THINK ABOUT

- How do you feel as you read this introduction? Can you identify some of your immediate emotions?
- What money-related issues come to mind that you would like to spend more time exploring?
- What issues might you discuss with someone else, and with whom?
- What issues might you think you could never discuss with someone else?
- What topics will you include in a letter to your money?
- How do you describe your relationship with your money?
- What questions do you hope to have answered as you read this book?

PART I:
Where We Find Ourselves

I invite you to take a journey with me to understand your relationship with money—where you learned the emotional and practical skills you use: those that serve you well, those you would like to revisit, those you might have missed learning—and, most importantly, how you can take an inner journey to attain financial wellness. We will start you on a path to change the unhealthy ways you think about money and prevent you from passing them along to other people you influence. You will build a path toward peace around finances that will calm your anxiety, build your confidence, and create a friendly relationship that gives you the power to take control of your money, rather than have your money control you.

Chapter 1

How Did We Get Here?

You might have heard the story about the little boy who asked, "Mommy, where did I come from?" His mother took a deep breath, thinking he seemed a bit young to be asking the question she thought he was asking. She calibrated her answer to make it as age-appropriate as possible. Remembering that she'd read about the importance of capturing the moment when children are ready to hear answers, she launched into a light version of the birds-and-the-bees story. When she stopped talking, he looked at her with a blank stare and replied, "But Mark says he's from Cleveland, and I'm wondering where I came from."

And so it is that I have three versions of "How did we get here?" stories to tell you. First, I'll share with you how I got here, literally, to Princeville, Kaua'i, where I have written this book, and then how you and I came to this place together to discuss your relationship with your money. And finally, how did we get here as an American society that tends to struggle when we discuss money, which, at its core, is a made-up concept that is used to facilitate a simple transactional exchange of goods and services for digital bits and pieces of paper. But, of course, we all know it's so much more than that.

How Did I Get Here?

In late October 2018, my son, Charles, took me to the Hawaiian island of Kaua'i to celebrate my recent birthday. On the last day of our long weekend on the island, we sat at a picnic table near the South Shore town of Po'ipū. Feeling the mist of the ocean wash over us as we watched the Spouting Horn blowhole erupt, we munched on snacks and wrote in our journals. As I reflected on our magical four days on the island, I made a written declaration that would change my life: *As we've experienced the majesty of this island, I have come to a decision that I will either live here or I will die.*

On November 6, 2019—almost exactly one year later—my flight from San Jose, California (SJC), landed at LIH, the primary airport for Kaua'i. I had followed through with my declaration so that I could write this book. When I'd made that declaration, I had no idea how I would afford living here, but my resolve wasn't mere words. To me, it was a live-or-die situation. Or, in the vernacular of Elle Luna's seminal book, *The Crossroads of Should and Must*, it was my "Must." Elle's book, I might add, had called to me from the library of the Airbnb where Charles and I stayed during our visit in 2018, as much as if it had vocal cords to be able to say, "Choose me!" I could never have imagined the ways the book would open my eyes to the magical path that would lay the groundwork during that year that separated my declaration and my departure. I came to write my first book; I stayed to live my best life.

One door after another opened so that by July I had engaged a book-writing coach, who suggested that I create a vision board in the form of a monthly timeline of what needed to happen to make my dream become a reality. I included a detailed list of requirements to enable my move. Even though I don't draw stick figures well, I drew a semblance of an airplane, a palm tree, and ocean waves over my targeted departure date of November 1. As things unfolded, the date moved to November 6, but it had all started with trusting a plan that nurtured my dream and brought me to a decision that would change my life. Ashima Sarin describes in *108 Blessings* exactly what had happened: "For our dreams to come true, we must first believe in their validity, fall in love with them, and hold their hands to their fruition."[1]

I also held tightly to my favorite quote from Ralph Waldo Emerson, because I know to the core of my being the depths of its truth: "Once you make a decision, the universe conspires to make it happen."

How Did *You* Get Here?

And now to the more important matter at hand—how did you get here? To this place where you're exploring how to:

- overcome your fear around money
- discover the power within you to free yourself from financial anxiety
- invest in your future so that you have peace around your finances

- trust that you can manage your money and control your spending

Obviously, I don't know your personal situation to be able to answer these questions for you, but we'll look at how others got here to see how their experiences map onto yours. From working with three generations of several families, I have seen how ideas and anxiety around money most likely didn't begin with us, or even with our parents. I have seen evidence that the unresolved financial issues of our ancestors continue to impact us, either by way of family patterns and habits or beliefs that were passed from generation to generation. Until we recognize the effects of familial patterns around money and decide that we will be the generation that puts an end to their negative impact on our lives, we will continue trying to make those patterns work for us, even when they obviously don't. As a friend once described, we're trying to wear our favorite dress from age four on our fourteen-year-old body.

When people share their experiences around money with me, they often start with what was happening when the first generation of their immigrant family arrived by sea through Ellis or Angel Island, or by land from Mexico or Canada, often with little or no money. Or they talk about how their ancestors faced financial hardship trying to eke out a living in the interior of the country in the late 1800s or early 1900s. Others talk about living through the Great Depression as children or hearing their parents describe the financial hardships their family endured during their formative years.

Alternatively, maybe you come from a family that had enough, or even more than enough money to live comfortably, yet you experienced money as a source of conflict in your family home over how it would be spent or who made decisions around it. If you don't recall hearing stories about money within your family, you might want to find out more about what happened in previous generations to better understand a piece of the puzzle about what has brought you to thinking about money the way you do.

Perhaps a deeper look at my own history, exploration, and changes in thinking about money will give you a model to help you get in touch with how you might have arrived here. I know little of my own familial history prior to a wee bit about my great-grandparents. I know that I come from a line of scrappy women survivors, where the three previous generations of men in my family abandoned their wives and kids, leaving them with little to no financial or emotional support.

As a single woman who was responsible for her family's sustenance at the turn of the twentieth century, my great-grandmother Della found a way to provide for herself and her two children before her death when my grandmother, her daughter, was sixteen. Fast-forward to the Great Depression, when my grandmother worked two jobs to support herself and her two daughters after her husband left his family to sleep on a neighbor's screened-in porch while he moved to a different state to work with the Civilian Conservation Corps. He rarely sent money home and never returned to his family.

My mom followed in the footsteps of her mother and grandmother as a single mother of two who, by the age of nineteen, was divorced, with no financial support from her ex-husband and not even a high school education to enable getting a job that paid enough to feed her little family.

Still, these three generations all persevered to become strong, resourceful, and independent women who did the best they could to provide for their families.

As I think of the legacy I inherited, I realize that it took all the energy my ancestors had to survive daily living. Therefore, they had no time or capacity to resolve the emotional issues that would be transferred from one generation to the next. This accumulation left a great deal of financial baggage for me to unpack. I've worked diligently to change my patterns around money from those I inherited to avoid passing along the pathologies of my past to my children. As my life circumstances have gone through extreme peaks and valleys, I suspect that my financial situation has changed more radically than most. In the process, my kids have experienced firsthand the consequences of both affluence and financial insecurity. Even though I've made progress, I've unfortunately left plenty of emotional work for the next generation to resolve. Still, I think I can safely say that my children have the benefit of having the tools to handle whatever twists and turns their financial lives might take.

It's taken the greater part of my life to understand, but with professional therapy and self-help work, I now know that I spent most of my life feeling like I needed to earn my place in this world to justify the space I took and resources I consumed. I believed that my value as a human being was determined by the amount of effort I put into making a contribution to society. Just as generations before me, I did whatever work it took to survive, justifying my existence throughout the stages of my life, striving relentlessly to be my best, whether working diligently in school to make good grades while having leadership roles in extracurricular activities, working to earn a livable salary, buying my first home at the age of nineteen, going to a prestigious university at the age of forty to get both bachelor's and master's degrees, serving on community and school boards, or owning a business whose payroll supported sixteen employees and their families. It's not lost on me that I believed my value came from my work efforts, rather than from whatever end result I accomplished.

Scarcity

When I was in my early forties, I was introduced to the term "scarcity mentality" while reading Stephen Covey's book *The 7 Habits of Highly Effective People.* I'd grown up knowing the feeling of scarcity to the core of my being, but Covey provided a name for it. Others have written about the concept, but it was his explanation that created a watershed moment in my life. I don't remember his exact words, but I internalized them in a way that made sense to me. I saw the universe as a place of scarcity, where life is one big pie, and if others take a slice, that leaves less pie for me. The financial circumstances of my ancestors and painful memories around money from my childhood made my dedication to scarcity understandable, even though it didn't serve me well.

I had no trouble rationally understanding the conceptual difference between scarcity mentality and its opposite, "abundance mentality," a philosophy that there's plenty of pie to go around for all of us, and if we run out, we'll make more pie. Though I attained considerable wealth for a time in my life, being able to have things and experiences to improve my quality of life beyond my wildest imagination, I operated from a core belief of scarcity. I could enjoy the benefits of wealth, but at the same time, I couldn't overcome my fear of losing them.

I found it impossible to internalize a sense of abundance, which to me meant having enough money to live my everyday life without anxiety around money. Even though I could easily pay bills and buy pretty much whatever I wanted, the anxiety remained. Seeing the world as abundant was a concept beyond anything I could imagine ever experiencing. The lens of scarcity created my worldview that defined a way of life for me. It was the pattern I'd always known, which made it comfortable in a distorted, unhealthy way.

My belief that I would never have enough money to feel secure was central to my personal identity. When we have a mindset of scarcity, it reaches other areas of our lives beyond finances, i.e., time, energy, health, well-being, attention, love, approval, and acceptance, to name a few. I now understand how I absorbed the fears and insecurity around money from my mother, grandmother, and great-grandmother that haunted me until I changed my thinking.

How do we move from a deeply seated belief that we must take what we can get to protect ourselves in a resource-limited world to an understanding that we can take what we need and want, and there will still be enough "pie" for all of us? Only after I internalized the inherent meaning of abundance did my understanding shift. The resulting change in my appreciation for abundance, beyond just the financial, created a message of hope that I want to share with you. This is the mantra by which I live today:

I release the chains of Scarcity and
replace them with the fruits and joys of
Abundance that are mine to claim.

I find that my attitude of abundance begets more abundance like a magnet draws iron toward it. Scarcity truly felt like I was constantly constricted by chains, without having enough money to cover basic needs, go where I wanted to go, get what I wanted to have, or even eat what I wanted to eat, particularly as a child. My childhood as a financial "have-not" seemed to be my destiny. As an adult, when I no longer lived a life of uncertainty and poverty, my core beliefs didn't adjust to my financial reality. Even though I could order whatever I wanted on a menu, buy what I wanted to sustain the quality of life I enjoyed, travel internationally, live in a house that our daughter's friends called a "mansion," and drive any cars I wanted, I approached life as if the pie were limited. And then, one day not that long ago, something clicked inside my mind, and my thinking changed. I dared to dream, and the more I dreamed, the more creativity I had to experience abundance in my life.

I relate to the way Ashima Sarin describes abundance in *108 Blessings*:

> We are all waiting recipients of unlimited abundance. It is our birthright like air or water. If we live as if we are deserving of it, then we will receive it. If we believe it is ours and give with as much joy as we receive it with, it will be ours and ours forevermore. But if we believe that we are not worthy, it will not stay. **For fear of loss is a self-fulfilling prophecy and what we are afraid to lose, we will. Abundance only stays with those who welcome it with open arms like a long-lost friend.** If we ask for what is ours and give knowing we have enough, then we are rich in the truest sense of the word.[[2]; emphasis mine]

When we experience fear around having enough money to meet our basic needs, or losing what we have acquired, it's hard to imagine having a life where Sarin's words could be true. Our worldview requires a scarcity mentality to support our self-image. I know this feeling because I lived with this same belief for most of my life. Still, I can assure you from my own experience that Sarin's promise is true. As I think about what changed for me, I'm convinced that it began with investigating the source of my fears and beliefs around money and what had to happen to let them go. And so it is that I want to share my story and those of others in this book to help you do the same so that you can have inner peace around your finances on your journey toward financial wellness.

How Did *We* Get Here?

And finally, how did we, as an American society, get here—where we struggle to discuss what, at its core, is a simple transactional exchange of goods and services for digital bits and pieces of paper, more commonly known as "money"? When we consider the functional reality of money, that's all it is. And yet, we all know it's so much more than that.

Among other things, it's a measuring stick often used to assess many different aspects of life, such as evidence of well-being, or a person's perceived "worth," or lack thereof. It signals societal status and opens doors to a multitude of opportunities for both ourselves and our families, including the availability of higher education, which often opens us to additional advancement. It also serves as emotional currency that impacts our meaningful relationships, and it can be a source of frustration and misery, whether we have it or we don't. It can be a source of joy and disappointment, delight and heartache, harmony and conflict, meaningful experiences and the lack thereof, connection and distance, security and insecurity, opportunity and disadvantage, adventure and caution, success and failure, safety and danger, comfort and suffering—and your list will surely include others.

So, why is it so hard to talk about money? What about it puts a knot in our stomachs, gives us headaches, makes our palms sweat or our chests clench, and makes some of us want to do just about anything other than think or talk about it? We'll devote the rest of our time together to helping you learn how to find the source of your pain and make peace with your money.

SOMETHING TO THINK ABOUT

- How would you describe your worldview around scarcity and abundance?
- What evidence do you have that your ancestors' beliefs around money influence your own thinking, patterns, and behavior?
- If you have difficulty talking about money, can you identify why that might be?
- If you were to talk about money with someone, who would that be?
- What comes to mind when you describe what money means to you?
- In what ways do you use money to measure other people or things?

Chapter 2

How to Shift Your Thinking

It seemed to me that my family's lot in life was to struggle so that we could prove we had the stamina to survive. Doing without equated to an honorable way of life. If I were to remain loyal to my family of origin, I thought I needed to maintain the belief that I would continue my family's legacy of scarcity. The idea that I could live from an attitude of abundance reminded me of my mom's oft-used admonition: "Don't get too big for your britches." I had to decide whether staying loyal to my heritage was more important than having the abundant life I wanted—enough to write, that day in 2018:

I will live here, or I will die.

When the consequence of not changing my core belief was experienced as a precursor to my own death, making a change became life saving. As I heard Leo Buscaglia say in a video many decades ago, "Anything that is learned can be unlearned." I was weary of living a life of fear around money, believing no amount of money would be enough for me to feel safe and secure, and that I couldn't overcome generations of evidence that scarcity was our family's destiny. My belief was so deeply entrenched that when things were going well and I should have realistically felt financially secure, I dreaded the proverbial shoe that I believed would surely drop. And it seemed as if it always did. I now believe that my impending downfall was a result of exactly what Ashima Sarin describes, that abundance would not stay because I didn't welcome it with open arms. And following Buscaglia's observation, I started my path to unlearn what I had learned. When we investigate our interpretation of stories we heard and events we experienced as kids, we can begin to understand how we think about money, how we came to our beliefs, and how we can change them.

We can understand how specific experiences shaped our ancestors' psyches and see how they came to some of their beliefs—beliefs that might have served them in their situation but most likely don't fit our lives today, beliefs that were often unknowingly and unintentionally passed on and absorbed by us. For generations in tribal, agrarian, and industrial societies, getting through daily life took all their time and energy, so people weren't thinking about ways to better understand their own behavior, improve their quality of life, or reflect on the ideas they were passing to their children. I doubt that many people were talking to their therapists about money during the early days of psychotherapy in 1950s America. And yet, based on my admittedly limited experience, many—if not most—people seem to have entrenched beliefs that cause them untold discomfort, pain, and sometimes trauma around money that could have been resolved had they spent time and effort seeking to understand their relationship with money or discussing these feelings with their therapist or others.

As I think of my own childhood in a home where finances were always at the center of my mom's thinking, my understanding has helped me have compassion for some of her struggles around money. When she was six years old in the 1930s, she developed pneumonia and nearly died. Living in rural western Oklahoma, she was taken a long distance from home to the next town that was large enough to have a hospital, where she was treated in an experimental apparatus called an "iron lung." Trapped alone in the device for weeks, she had only occasional visits from her parents because it was the Depression and they had to stay home to keep their teaching jobs. Also, they didn't have gas rations that would allow them to drive often to the town where she was hospitalized, so she scarcely saw her family for the months she was in the hospital. She told the story many times of blaming herself for the family's furniture being repossessed after she returned home. She described her vivid memory of feeling guilty as she stood at the front door waving goodbye to their refrigerator, watching as it was taken away on the back of the repossessor's truck. For the rest of her life, she struggled emotionally when buying a refrigerator. Remembering an experience that was obviously fraught with pain, invariably, she wouldn't like the refrigerator she'd chosen—and it always prompted the retelling of this childhood experience, often through tears.

I find it fascinating that Mom rarely spoke of what could only have been a terrifying experience of being in the iron lung. Instead, she poured her memories into blaming herself for their family's financial struggles . . . in the middle of the Depression, when nearly everyone had financial difficulties, with a father who eventually lost his job! It seemed that her memory had no context by which to understand the timing of the events, and blaming herself created the punishment she seemed to feel she deserved.

Trauma Transfer

I know few details of my family history, but I know a great deal about the financial trauma that was transferred through the generations. I know that my grandmother grew up with a father who went on drinking binges until he ran out of money, returning home to get more from his wife so he could leave again. I don't know how my great-grandmother earned money, but I believe the financial trauma of my great-grandparents was passed down through subsequent generations to me. And I know that in the next generation, my grandfather was fired from his job as a schoolteacher because he didn't pay his bills in a timely manner, which was deemed a lack of good moral character. My grandmother worked two jobs, as a schoolteacher during the day and a waitress at night, leaving her preteen daughters to fend for themselves while she worked. And I know that in the next generation, my mother tried to care for my brother and me with what she could earn with a ninth-grade education and no husband or child support. I can only guess at the extent of suffering and fear caused by financial insecurity for these women—my mother, grandmother, and great-grandmother. I also know the intention that has been required to keep from passing along my history and trauma around money to my children.

I tell you my history to explain how deeply rooted my trauma around money was in my psyche. If I could overcome my fear of scarcity, I know you can too. Shifting my thinking about money took a long time to contemplate and grasp, and even longer to internalize. However, I now understand that it's taken every experience of my life—those that I remember with fondness and joy, as well as those that come with considerable pain—for me to become the person who believes in abundance that I am today. The same is true for every one of us. Each and every experience we've lived has served a purpose in shaping the person we are at this current moment in our lives. Let's hold that thought, resting with the truth of that fact without letting our ego do what it does naturally—jump immediately to judgment. You might want to say it out loud to emphasize it to yourself:

Each and every experience I've lived
has served a purpose in bringing me to the place
where I am at this moment in my life.

This instant, when you're reading this book, is one moment in your lifetime, and it will impact your future life in ways you cannot know now. I encourage you to relish in this moment—alone with your thoughts, living in your beautiful state of being—while you are not performing any of the roles you have in relationship to others.

The accumulation of every experience has not only brought us to this moment; it also has the potential to provide us with insight, understanding, and wisdom. And so it is that we can appreciate all our previous life experiences, some with pebbles in our shoes that have caused us to stumble, and some that allowed us to skip through life with clarity of direction. Whatever we experienced in those moments, the vision of hindsight lets us see the value of the purpose they served, if we're open to revisiting them. As we go through the stories ahead, even those that may trigger painful memories, I hope you'll be grateful for whatever you have gained from each and every one of your life experiences.

SOMETHING TO THINK ABOUT

- If you have living parents, grandparents, or other family members from previous generations, what would you like to ask them about familial ideas around money?
- How deeply entrenched in family traditions are the messages you think you must follow in order to be accepted by your family?
- As you think about your ancestors, what evidence do you see of their beliefs around money reflected in your thinking, patterns, and behavior?
- What are some ways you would like to change your relationship with money?

Chapter 3

Let's Talk About Money

In this chapter, we'll cover:

- some of the many reasons why talking about money is difficult
- how the messages we received from our family about money continue to influence us
- benefits we might expect from doing the hard work to better understand ourselves
- how money is used to convey messages that may or may not be received accurately

By virtue of your selecting this book, I'm assuming some things about you. Let's see if they're correct. First, you are less than satisfied with your relationship with money—and that might be a gross understatement. Second, you find it difficult to discuss money, or maybe even to think about it. And third, you likely have a visceral bodily reaction to the "should" messages in your mind around money. You know the ones (this list is by no means exhaustive; these are just a few of the comments I've heard from friends and clients):

- I should open my mail.
- I should pay my bills.
- I should have a budget.
- I should know where I stand financially.
- I should know more about our family's finances.
- I should have a personal relationship with our professional financial and legal advisors.
- I should be more involved in our investments.
- I should care about our finances.
- I should know where to find information if my partner dies.
- I should know where we have bank accounts and if we have a safe deposit box.
- I should have a will and/or trust.
- I should know if we're in debt, and if so, how much we owe and to whom.
- I should know how much my spouse/partner earns.
- I should know how much I spend.
- I should know where my money goes.
- I should know what we spend on the kids.
- I should know how we're going to pay for our kids' college.
- I should know if we have retirement accounts and how much we have saved.
- I should know if my parents are going to need financial help someday.
- I should gather information to have my taxes calculated.
- I should know what I'm signing when I sign our tax returns.

Before we look at some of the reasons why we think we have any of these "should" messages, let's take a few deep breaths and remember your purpose: to have a roadmap to guide you toward financial wellness. You're seeking a more healthy, peaceful, and constructive relationship with your finances—to move from angst about money to peacefulness and calm. Know that we're going to discover together how you can feel safe around working with your finances.

Sometimes I hear from clients that there are days when they can talk about money, and then there are others when they can't go to the dark place where it takes them emotionally. I truly get it; there are a whole lot of people for whom thinking about money is excruciatingly painful. Their pain, and possibly yours, is real and often physical. It is not to be discounted or glossed over. Looking the dragon in the mouth will provide a way out of the pain, whether you walk the path with me or with the help of a professional life coach or therapist, or both. I'd guess that money would be at or near the top of a list of topics therapists hear most often from clients, so remember that you are not alone.

I encourage you to be especially curious about topics that you might think are off-limits, possibly even taboo, in your own thoughts or discussions. Identify those aspects around your money that you find comfortable to discuss, and those you don't. Pay attention to what you're feeling in your body as certain thoughts cross your mind. Please keep in mind that our bodies react before our brains engage, especially when we're experiencing emotions such as fear, shame, and anxiety. A friend of mine sees colors that reveal her different emotions. These reactions provide signals that we should heed. Personally, when I come upon a topic that isn't comfortable to discuss, I literally feel a tightening in my chest, an internal mechanism that says, *Don't go there. It might not be safe.*

To help you enhance your relationship with your money, we'll look at:

- why and how you think and feel about your money and maybe that of others
- why you might struggle with both thinking and talking about it
- how you relate to money in ways that might not be obvious even to you
- the patterns you've developed around using it
- how you make financial decisions
- how and when you might want to discuss money with others

While it's important to unearth these emotions in order to uncover their sources, it's equally important to take care of yourself in the process—not to go down a dark hole that overwhelms you with painful memories and exacerbates your fear and anxiety. I encourage you to be tender, compassionate, and loving with yourself, and perhaps with your parents as well. Blaming yourself or others serves no benefit, and we do well to remember that in most cases, our parents were doing the best they knew how to do. They were following patterns they'd watched their parents use, and their parents had done the same with their parents. Those patterns might have worked for earlier generations, but they likely did not serve the next generation well, and yet, they were passed down. There's no one to blame for how we relate to money, neither our parents nor ourselves. Mistakes might have been made, but that's all they were—mistakes.

It's also important that we allow ourselves to feel

whatever emotions we're experiencing. Let your tears flow when they come. Think of what we might tell a child we see sitting on a curb crying, as we put our arms around her: "Tell me about it, Sweetheart. What's making you cry?"

If you're someone who has a physical reaction to thinking about money, you likely experienced trauma around money that lingers in your body. Trauma that isn't dealt with stays with us until we work through it. If you're looking for a clue to the beginning of your difficult relationship with money, you might want to go back in the deep recesses of your childhood memories to find it.

Financial trauma could be a result of a lifetime of witnessing your parents being conflicted or having arguments around money, or perhaps one specific event that causes you to recoil when you recall it. Maybe you watched your parents struggle emotionally around money, or perhaps they didn't discuss it in your presence, but you felt the undercurrent in your home as you grew up. You might have grown up with an ongoing fear of financial insecurity, perhaps in a home with a parent who couldn't keep a job. You might have lived in a home with substance abuse or grown up in a home where the family business created a sense of "feast or famine," as mine did when I was a teenager. After my mom married my stepdad, who had a small business, the menu for our evening meals depended on which customers' payments were waiting at the post office box—or weren't. My heart tightens even now as I remember Mom going to the post office twice a day to see if a particular check had arrived. When a large check was there, we celebrated by eating steak for dinner, and when no promised check arrived, Mom made do with whatever was in the pantry, often cream chipped beef on toast, fried Spam, or pinto beans.

Perhaps you grew up with a sense that money was the unspoken elephant in the room. Kids are incredibly adept at picking up vibes. Maybe your parents didn't know the amount each other earned. You might be surprised to know that I hear comments like "I don't know what my husband makes"—yes, still today in America. Interestingly, I've never heard the comment, "I don't know what my wife makes," even though, in 2018, 43 percent of Americans reported not knowing how much money their spouses earn.[1] This percentage makes me think many husbands also don't know what their wives earn, and from experience, I know some people who don't know what they themselves earn. Furthermore, perhaps you observed how gender inequality around money impacted your parents' relationship, possibly causing arguments or creating distance between them. We'll explore in more detail how money and gender relate in Chapter Eight.

Additionally, you most likely have not had the benefit of being formally taught how to manage your money. I've only met a handful of people who said one or both of their parents intentionally taught them about finances, specifically mentioning handling credit cards, learning about real estate and investments, paying bills, and tracking their spending. Some public schools have begun to incorporate financial literacy courses into their curricula, and private schools might be more likely to help prepare their typically wealthier students for adulthood, but nationally, schools tend to be cutting back on subjects that used to be considered important, such as art, music, and physical education. In financially strapped schools, I find it ironic that financial literacy is another subject they don't think they can afford to teach.

So, with the assumption that most of us weren't specifically taught about finances, let's remember that we all *learned* something—probably more than we realize—in the homes where we were raised. Regardless of what your parents might have intended to teach, you probably also learned significantly more than they realized about their values and ideas around money. When we think about the way we learned about money, for many—if not most—of us, the process didn't provide the information we needed to feel confident in our ability to manage our financial lives.

If you're a parent reading this, I'd be remiss not to add the number of times I've heard parents describe how they tried to teach their kids about money, and the kids made it clear that they weren't interested—or perhaps were so uncomfortable with the subject that they made it next to impossible for the parents to even have simple discussions. Some kids seem to be hard-wired not to think about money, or they have a visceral reaction to most, if not all, aspects of it. And especially for some teenagers, the last person they want to discuss something that's hard to talk about with is their parent. For some kids, spending is painful. For others, *not* spending is painful. Some struggle with the logistics of handling an allowance or keeping track of their money. They don't want to hear the messages their parents try to teach them, information they will need to know as they become adults. Some seem to be little Peter Pans, wanting to avoid the responsibilities that come with growing up, which is now called "adulting." We'll look at more specific ways kids struggle with financial matters when we talk about kids and money in Chapter Fifteen.

The messages we left home with as young adults, however we learned them, informed our relationship with money, our feelings toward it (both positive and negative), and our social interactions around it, whether with family, with friends, in intimate relationships, or in business. Maybe you grew up hearing your parents talk about other people in ways that told you their underlying opinions—perhaps how Uncle Harry, the black sheep of the family, "never had two nickels to rub together," their way of saying his lack of money meant they didn't value what he had accomplished in his life. Or Cousin Joan, whose kids got your hand-me-down clothes "because her deadbeat husband won't pay child support."

When you think about how you define money, your parents' messages likely become your self-talk. Perhaps you remember arguments whenever they spoke of money. Maybe your mother confided in you that she used money to "get back" at your dad for distancing himself from her and the family, working long hours, drinking, or having an extramarital affair. Did your mother get "the silent treatment" and a look of disapproval when she came home with shopping bags? Perhaps, like my friend Frankie, your mom took you on all-day shopping sprees, saying, "Let's get in trouble," laughing about how angry her husband would be when the ensuing credit card statement would arrive. This experience influenced Frankie's life to the extent that she has difficulty with spending issues, calling herself a shopaholic.

As you think about the subliminal messages you absorbed as a child and consider how they've influenced your current thinking, you might ask your parents if the messages you remember hearing reflect their underlying beliefs about those same situations. In many instances, when we test our understanding of our memories, especially of events that happened long ago, we learn new information that sometimes alters how we think about whatever happened, or we're able to let go of the memory altogether because it no longer serves us. Reprocessing and testing the validity of these memories can help us better understand our thinking around money.

Another way to consider our relationship with money is to think about the emotional ways we use it beyond its transactional value. The list is long as to the ways money is used to create emotional currency between people. For example, gifts might be the language of love for the partner or spouse who buys them or the one who wants (or demands) to receive them. Gifts convey various messages—perhaps love, care, celebration, duty, expectation, peace offering, or a request for forgiveness. When you're the recipient of a gift that is intended to convey a message, you're often left to interpret that message through the lens of your own life experiences. Perhaps the giver has difficulty finding words, so they (and it's almost always *he*) assume their gift will say the words for them. They may not understand that the gift alone doesn't accomplish their intended purpose and might even send a significantly different message from the intended one when it's not accompanied by words, especially if the gift is a plastic laundry basket, like the one my mom received for her anniversary one year.

When couples don't share gift-giving as a common currency, the results can be painful, as we'll see when we meet my friends, Steve and Nancy.

››› *Steve and Nancy*

> Steve and Nancy have endured a marriage filled with arguments and anguish over four decades of holidays and "special" days together. When we look at why this might be, we see that their different childhood experiences created significantly different feelings around gift giving. Steve sees special dates as "Hallmark-induced commercialism," where he's

expected to adhere to an American advertising machine's creation that he adamantly refuses to participate in. Further exacerbating his reactions to special days, as the oldest of four children, he experienced each of his birthdays as being less important as each new sibling was born. The year he turned ten, his mother brought home a cake and gifts to celebrate—exactly one month before his actual birthday. After she smiled and set a cake with burning candles in front of him, he asked, "Whose birthday is it?" to which she replied, "Yours!" He said, "No, Momma, my birthday is the fifth of next month. Today is August 5th." Today, she sends birthday cards belatedly to her children. Steve tells me that getting a birthday card from his mother in November, when his birthday was in September, has little significance beyond irritation. It's not hard to understand why he enjoys neither giving nor receiving birthday gifts. His painful memories impact his ideas around giving gifts for any occasion.

His wife, Nancy, on the other hand, enjoys celebrating holidays and finds delight in all aspects of gift-giving, from selection to wrapping to presenting gifts to the recipient. When they were dating, Nancy had great fun preparing for Steve's birthday. She watched in anticipation as he unwrapped the large box she'd handed him, only to find a gift and a smaller box inside. He continued opening several smaller boxes, each with a gift inside, until he reached the smallest one, which contained the most special gift: diamond-studded cufflinks. His reaction was neither what she'd hoped for nor might have reasonably expected. Decades after this happened, she teared up as she relayed the story to me of how devastated she felt when Steve didn't appear to enjoy her gifts or the efforts she'd made to present them in her unique way.

Nancy quickly learned that being in a relationship with Steve would mean she would experience neither the joy of giving him gifts, through which she hoped to convey her love for him, nor the joy of receiving gifts from him. With few exceptions, on those special dates when he's given her a gift, his choices have conveyed his sense of obligation more than a message that he's thought about what she might like or enjoy. And on many birthdays, anniversaries, and traditional gift-exchanging days, she's gotten no gift at all. While she continued to give him gifts for many years, she now tells me she "no longer bothers." Even though Nancy knows that Steve's language of love clearly is not gift-giving, she experiences his attitude around gifts as a lack of appreciation or willingness to demonstrate his love in a meaningful way. Today, Nancy gives herself gifts on her special days, often making an effort to be out of town on those days so that she isn't reminded of the pain she expects to experience if she were to stay in town. Steve's efforts to show his love through earning a good living that provides well for their family, taking care of the cars, and planning fun excursions and trips seem to be lost on her.

On the other end of the spectrum, some couples have a joint language of love that includes gift-giving, and the message is perfectly understood and appreciated, as exemplified by Jeremy and Cassie.

››› *Jeremy and Cassie*

Jeremy loves giving gifts, especially to the love of his life, Cassie. He enjoys thinking about what might please her, searching for just the right style and color. As he knows she enjoys wearing jewelry, he is a good customer of their small-town jeweler. Likewise, Cassie knows how much Jeremy loves sports and gives him gifts that honor his passion. Gifts are a way they deepen their relationship, as they share a common currency.

Besides providing emotional currency between couples, what else is money? A formal, not very satisfying, definition from economists: Money is "something that serves as a medium of exchange, a unit of accounting, and a store of value."[2] This speaks to the purpose of money in a transactional sense, but not to the emotional experience that often accompanies it.

Some think of money as a tool to get what you want in life, as a means to an end. Others say it is energy that filters through the universe to provide for our every need. A Google search about money unearths trite comments such as:

- "Having good health or money isn't everything, but not having it is."
- "You don't need six-pack abs or ten million dollars to be happy, but it is worth learning the fundamentals of fitness and finance."
- "Money provides a margin of safety."
- Or the all-knowing words of Tevye in the movie *Fiddler on the Roof*, who wryly observes how society often treats wealth as

> a stand-in for wisdom: "When you're rich, they think you really know."

Throughout our time together, we'll explore ways money is used to convey messages we've internalized—often unknowingly—and those that are shared by our families, as well as by society in general. Perhaps a parent believes the long hours spent working to become a law partner are justified because their status and income will provide more opportunities and a better life for their children. Or a doctor who chooses to be on call on weekends may think the extra income is more beneficial to their family than the time they'd otherwise spend together. A high-tech startup founder who has gotten into the habit of rarely being home might believe their six-figure income conveys their love, protects the family's well-being, and provides the ability for them to do and have "nice things."

Money can also convey a pecking order and create divisions within families. A friend who has more money than her parents or siblings describes how the disparity in finances impacts even simple decisions. Recently, when her niece graduated from college, she planned to give her a gift of $100. When her brother and mother told her they were each giving $250, she felt like she needed to increase the amount of her gift since she has more financial resources than they do. She thought her family would think badly of her if she didn't give a gift that was at least the same amount as theirs. In other situations, those who have improved their financial standing in life over that of their family believe they've worked hard to better themselves and don't want to be thought of in the same light as less affluent members of their family.

››› *Frances and Jenny*

Frances was a successful single woman, having opened a personal training fitness center with the money she inherited after her young mother's death. She began experiencing fatigue and joint pain, which sometimes kept her from being able to work. As her symptoms worsened and doctors searched for a diagnosis, she had no energy to continue the business she loved. Eventually, she was diagnosed with an autoimmune disease that allowed her to get government disability payments.

While Frances struggled with her health and business, her sister, Jenny, had married a wealthy Texas oilman. Jenny and her husband bought a sprawling ranch and started their family, while Frances was struggling to pay her rent. Frances missed seeing Jenny and wanted to meet her newborn niece. When she scraped together enough money to make the trip to Texas, she was met by a different person from the sister she'd played with as kids. As she described her experience to me: "It felt like I wasn't good enough for her anymore. Maybe she thought I was going to ask to borrow money, so she put a wall between us."

Frances never learned what had happened to create a rift between them, but she got the distinct impression that her sister's new wealth created a need to distance herself from her "poor relations," as Jenny referred to Frances and their dad. Frances's health has continued to deteriorate to the extent that she will never be able to take long trips again. She's resigned herself to never seeing Jenny again, because Jenny has said she'll never return to their small hometown.

Hopefully, these stories will provide some food for thought to help you understand your thinking and expectations around money. As you reflect on ways your experiences are similar to or different from the ones you've just read about, you might want to make some notes about topics you'd like to explore. Perhaps you don't relate specifically to any of these examples, but a memory was triggered that you hadn't previously considered as being relevant to your feelings around money.

In whatever way you find helpful, I encourage you to begin identifying your own ways of thinking about money. In subsequent chapters, we'll look at different stories and situations you can use to deepen your understanding of how you think about money and the ways it impacts your life.

SOMETHING TO THINK ABOUT

- When you think about money, does your body react in a certain way?
- What specific messages do you carry from your parents around money?
- What would be included in your list of "shoulds" around money?
- As you read these stories, what memories come to mind?
- If you took a snapshot of your thinking about money, what would it include?
- What statement(s) would you have made about money before reading this chapter? How would they be different now?

Chapter 4

How to Talk with Others

As you consider discussing your thoughts, experiences, and decisions around money with other people, think about what you're okay with sharing. Be aware of the circumstances around having conversations that will accomplish your desired goals. The content of these conversations will vary with the degree of intimacy you have with your listener, the level of vulnerability you feel comfortable exposing, and the details you choose to disclose.

Trust your gut to decide what to include and to whom. Again, the type of relationship you have with your confidant will help inform your decisions about what you wish to discuss. You might want to have several shorter conversations rather than one longer one, and you might have more than a single confidant with whom you'd be comfortable sharing different aspects of your journey around money.

I encourage you to identify how your body reacts when you discuss something that feels uncomfortable and to be curious when you're feeling discomfort. At what point does your inner voice say, *Don't go there*? When considering what information you'd like to share, notice what provides a pathway into understanding yourself, even when the emotion is tied to a painful memory.

First and foremost, you need to be comfortable knowing that you can trust the other person to maintain confidentiality and be the listener *you* need. Therefore, you might want to first have a preliminary conversation with your confidant about your desire to discuss money. This will give you an opportunity to find out if they are open to discussing it in a way that will be helpful to you. And remember, if you've never discussed money with anyone before, you and your partner or friend are in uncharted waters that could get choppy.

As you think about having conversations around money, you'll want to find out if your partner or friend can discuss money in a way that feels safe to you. Ask your listener if they would be open to talking with you about money. Then, tell them what you'd like to hear from them after you share your thoughts. Decide in advance if you want them just to listen and acknowledge that you've been heard, to provide an opportunity for you to "think out loud," or if you want them to tell you how their experiences around money are similar to or different from yours. Tell them whether or not you're seeking their advice, so they know how to respond in a way that's beneficial to you.

As an example of how you might approach the topic with a friend or partner, the conversation could go something like this:

> "I've been exploring what I think about money, and I'd like to chat about my ideas with you. I'm not looking for advice, but it would be helpful to share my thinking and hear what you think, too, if you'd be open to that."

Something to consider before broaching the topic of money with another person: The size of our account balances and debt tends to get tangled up with our sense of how we see ourselves and how we think others might perceive us, if they only knew our truth. Before deciding what details to share, think about what you're comfortable revealing about your situation. For example, are you concerned that if you reveal the amount of your income to your confidant, they might assign their own meaning to it and perhaps view you in a different light?

Perhaps you think they'll interpret your income as evidence of the extent to which you are valued in your workplace, something they might equate with the value you contribute to your family and community. Or, perhaps you're concerned that you'll be perceived as bragging and feel guilty that you're doing better financially than they are, or better than many of your peers. Possibly you fear that you'll be seen by your confidant as irresponsible if you reveal that you're in debt to your eyeballs, perhaps with tens or even hundreds of thousands of dollars in student loan debt or maxed-out credit cards, or that your work is of lesser value because you earn less than they do.

Our fear of feeling shame weighs heavily on our ability to talk openly and honestly about money, especially if we don't think we manage it well. We often assume others are doing a better job with their money than we are. The truth is that our struggle with money is a secret that many experience but few are open to discussing with others. Making peace with our money is an act of courage, and courage happens as a result of facing our fears.

Let's look at some of the people with whom you might want to have conversations around money. One of the first places you might notice discomfort around money happens as you explore dating relationships. You might feel a twinge as your dating partner suggests an expensive ski trip that is beyond your comfort level. Do you share that discomfort or go along with it because you're not ready to reveal your personal financial situation? At what point does it feel safe to talk about money? By the time you're in an intimate relationship, you'll likely find it helpful to explore how your ideas and those of your partner are similar or conflict, why that might be so, and how those differences or similarities impact your relationship, or possibly will later. Because most of us only know what we learned from growing up in our immediate family, we sometimes aren't aware of the extent of differences that are possible among families when thinking about money. We often assume that other people think the same way we do because we haven't had conversations to learn that our family's way of doing things is different from that of others. In Chapter Fourteen, we'll discuss partners and money in greater depth, where I'll tell you stories that will shed light on the importance of discussing money with your significant other, partner, or spouse.

Our immediate family is a resource for understanding how we think about money—especially our siblings, who likely were close to our age when we experienced events in our family home that informed our financial thinking. Still, it's not uncommon for siblings who shared the same family experiences to have different memories of particular events, which often result in significantly different beliefs about money. Siblings often have vast differences in how they make financial choices.

I also encourage you to talk to your extended family—your grandparents, parents, aunts, and uncles—about the ancestry of money in your family to learn where some of your beliefs and ideas might have originated. Look for patterns that cross generations, and remember that we, especially as young children, identify with our parents most often through our observations of their behavior. We assign meaning to their attitudes, emotions, and behavior, rather than confirming the accuracy of our perceptions. Therefore, as children, we are left to make sense of complex issues with our own immature processing abilities. As young adults, we're left trying to grow in financial independence, but we've been planted in soil that includes stones of painful experiences and memories from our childhood, as well as those of our parents, and sometimes their parents.

Now, with your own thoughts and memories and the newly acquired information gleaned from conversations with others, you are ready to explore how these beginnings will create a roadmap for your path to a powerful, healthier, more constructive, and peaceful relationship with your money.

SOMETHING TO THINK ABOUT

- As you read this chapter, what thoughts are triggered about discussing money with someone?
- When you think about having conversations around money, who comes to mind as someone you'd be comfortable talking to?
- What are your earliest memories of money?
- What is your first painful memory around money?
- What financial topics would you be comfortable discussing with someone else?
- Who in your family would you like to know more about in relation to money? What questions would you like to ask them?
- What issues have you never thought about before, but after reading this chapter, you'd like to investigate further?
- Who might be a good resource to help you find the answers to your questions?

PART II: How We Think About Money

In this section, we'll look at specific issues that significantly influence our emotions around money:

- how financial stress impacts other parts of our lives
- how our thoughts about money inform our ideas about our personal identities and how we present ourselves to the world
- how our process for making financial decisions might be different from the processes we use to make other decisions
- how gender income inequality has far-reaching implications at both personal and societal levels
- how the way we earn money influences our ideas around money

- how determining if something is a "need" or a "want" impacts how we think about spending money on it
- how we identify "enough"
- how we think about budgeting
- how the cyclical nature of finances can turn our world upside down

Chapter 5

When Financial Stress Feels Overwhelming

You might find it surprising to know that habits, patterns, and experiences around money can create so much stress that I've been invited to therapy sessions with clients. In some cases, clients hope my reflections on their spending habits will help their therapist better understand how their emotional issues with money play out in other aspects of their lives. One client invited me to several therapy sessions so I could share my observations about her struggles with her own spending habits and ideas around money. In another case, a client asked me to help his therapist understand the extent to which giving money to his grown children was putting his own financial security at risk.

My Story

I will spend much of this chapter telling you my own story around financial stress, as stress is something we each experience in our own way. I can see evidence of clients' stress, but I can't describe exactly what they're feeling. I *can* share with you how I lived with financial stress throughout most of my life, from the ancestral inheritance of a scarcity mentality and insecurity over basic necessities of everyday life to the absorption of my mom's fears and anxieties over money as I experienced them as her child.

I've never considered not working for the rest of my life. Working has always been a given, as I've never seen anyone in my family retire. After my first ill-fated marriage at eighteen and divorce at twenty-one, I put my financial life in order. Once I was free from having to consider my husband's opinions, constraints, and ego, I was like a team of horses chomping at the bit to create the financial life I wanted. For a short time, I felt financially secure, with a salary that provided more than adequately for my every need, a comfortable balance in my checking account, a significant savings account, a wardrobe of expensive clothes, a new top-of-the-line car I'd bought with literal cash (I had great fun counting out hundred-dollar bills on the salesman's desk), and a completely remodeled house with everything new, from furnishings to landscaping, and mortgage payments of less than $100/month. No, that's not a typo, as I had bought a tiny two-bedroom post-war house in Oklahoma.

When I married Kent, my second husband, I thought my fears around money would end, but that was not to be the case. I had worked since I was too young to do so legally, having first worked in a privately owned clothing boutique that didn't mind bending the rules by paying my salary in cash (so as not to have to provide the government with documentation of my age).

Kent and I didn't discuss money before we married, less than two years after my divorce. I made considerable attribution errors in assuming that his habits around money meant he had significant financial resources. Within a couple of years of our marriage, the scarcity mentality that was buried in my soul reared its head once more. Even after a few years that provided evidence of our financial security, I couldn't shake my underlying fears that I now know resulted from my scarcity mentality. If I'd known then what was to come, I would have realized my intuition was correct.

A couple of years into our marriage, Kent came home from work and announced that he had told his boss (who happened also to be his dad) that he was leaving their family's business. We hadn't discussed that he was considering this important change in his livelihood—*our* livelihood—and how it would affect us or our soon-to-be expanding family, as I was six months pregnant. I don't recall that we'd ever talked about how long I'd take off work for maternity leave, but after he quit his job, I believed I had no choice but to return to work soon after our daughter's birth. Fortunately, the owner of the small, family-owned business where I worked put a crib in my office so I could take our daughter to work. This convenience allowed me to spend time caring for her while, no doubt, doing a less-than-stellar job.

Kent always had big dreams, coupled with unmitigated confidence and chutzpah. Rather than going through traditional routes to find a new job, he wrote letters to industry leaders whom he admired after reading articles about them in *Fortune* magazine. He assumed his attitude would get him interviews with CEOs of major companies. The fact that Kent had no skills specific to their industries did not deter him. He thought his passion for their vision would be sufficient to spark their interest in hiring him. He received some cordial, hand-signed letters from rather important people from his efforts (as sending letters was how business was done in the mid-1970s), but no interview requests.

As the due date of our baby's birth grew closer and our bank account balance dwindled without the monthly addition of his paycheck, my fear increased. I worked until about a week before our daughter was born to continue receiving my small income for as long as possible.

Given that Kent had left a job in a wholesale carpet business that his grandfather had founded in the late 1940s, he went to the carpet capital of the world—Dalton, Georgia—to meet with Martin B. "Bud" Seretean. In 1965, Bud had been named the Outstanding Small Businessman in the Nation and he had recently sold his carpet company, Coronet Industries, to RCA, becoming their largest single shareholder.[1] Kent's father and grandfather had done business with Bud for many years, and his assistant scheduled a meeting with Kent, out of respect for his family name, I would guess. We didn't know how we would pay the American Express charge for his airline ticket to travel to meet Bud when the statement arrived, but Kent made the trip to Dalton on a wing and a prayer.

When Bud asked Kent what he wanted to do with his life, Kent gave a vague answer, something like, "I want to make a difference, but not in the carpet business." As Bud knew Kent's family history as a pillar in the carpet industry, he mentioned the size of the worldwide industry and asked if Kent thought he could find a place in an industry so large. Bud reminded him how he had a large Rolodex of contacts and knowledge of the industry.

Kent left Bud's office with a changed mind and enthusiasm for a future in the industry that had provided well for his grandparents and parents. Before driving to the Atlanta airport to catch a flight home, he stopped at a small carpet manufacturer housed in a repurposed chicken coop and asked if they had something he could sell. They cut a corner off a roll of carpet for him to take back to Oklahoma. He knew that if he could sell it quickly and be paid within the next month, we would be able to pay the credit card charge for his airline ticket and make our next month's house payment.

He shared the events of the past few hours on our drive home from the airport, informing me that he was going to start a new business selling carpet wholesale—and that he wanted me to be involved. We used our initials to come up with a name, KVTV (Kent Vickery Tari Vickery), even though it sounded like a television station's call-letters. We incorporated the business on August 16, 1976, a month before the birth of our daughter. We often remarked that we had two children in the same year—our daughter and our business.

With the piece of carpet he'd brought from Georgia, Kent sold several rolls of it to a carpet dealer who worked out of his garage in a rural town. Most importantly, the dealer would pay us when he took delivery, which is not typical payment terms in the industry. Kent had convinced the manufacturer to wait thirty days from the date of shipment for our payment to them, which gave us time to collect from our customer and pay the manufacturer. The profit we made and my salary were enough to pay our bills that month. Bud's advice served Kent well, as we consistently hit each of the sales milestones in a business plan he crafted during his flight home from Georgia.

I was able to leave my job after about a year and work full-time in our fledgling company, doing everything from administrative work to learning to drive a forklift with a carpet pole so I could run the warehouse and office during the day while Kent called on customers to generate sales. As we were a wholesale distributor, we bought carpet in large rolls and cut it to the sizes our retail dealers needed for specific jobs. After Kent ended his day of selling, we picked up our daughter from daycare on our way to a restaurant to eat dinner. Then we returned to the warehouse, where we worked late into the night cutting carpet to the sizes customers needed to pick up the following day. Night after night, our daughter played on rolls of carpet until she fell asleep. By the time we finished getting orders ready for the next day, we typically carried a sleeping child to the car to go home and start it all over again early the next day.

Over the course of ten years, our business thrived, and we were rewarded financially for the utterly insane hours we worked—seven days a week. Eventually, our business generated sizable profits that resulted in paying so much in income taxes that it felt like we were working for Uncle Sam. To reduce our burdensome tax liability, we bought an expensive home that provided a tax deduction in the days when average annual mortgage rates exceeded 16 percent. Maintaining our large home and meeting the monthly mortgage payments required us to work even longer hours, so that we had little time to swim in our pool or enjoy our wealth.

We took our daughter on weekend trips to Disneyland and other fun places and typically went to New York City every few months, but we could never be away from the business for more than three or four days at a time. Eventually, we had sixteen employees in three states and annual sales of $10 million—until the economy came to a screeching halt.

The price of oil drives the economy in Oklahoma, and that price collapsed in 1985 from $27/barrel to $13 in a matter of weeks. *The New York Times* ran an article titled "Desperation Descends on Oklahoma,"[2] which described what became the catalyst for the swift and devastating end of our business. After the infamous demise of Penn Square Bank, which held our operating loans, we transitioned to a New York bank whose representative soon thereafter told us he had instructions to "get out of Oklahoma at any cost." Within three months, the bank forced us and their other two largest Oklahoma customers to close our businesses in ways that didn't provide an opportunity to preserve our wealth. The businesses were all family-owned: a hundred-year-old candy company (Bunte Candies), a lumber company founded in 1933 (Caston Lumber), and our business that we'd invested every waking moment and nearly every penny earned for ten years to grow.

And so it was that every aspect of our world fell apart. By the time our business ended, we had another baby on the way, so our children created bookends to our business. It had been incorporated on August 16, 1976, and we turned the key to lock the door for the last time on August 16, 1986. As I sat in my office listening to the auctioneer sell the assets of our business, I once again feared the world I was bringing this new baby into. Even with all our financial success, the decade in between our children's births had done nothing to relieve my belief that my heart would always be filled with fear around money.

During the years of increasing affluence, with the accompanying societal trappings of wealth, I was exhausted from the work required to maintain our lifestyle. On many Sunday afternoons, I struggled with feelings of not wanting to go to the office but knowing I would pay dearly on Monday morning for not getting a jump start on my work for the week. I expended a lot of energy having a conflicted conversation with myself, oscillating between feeling guilty for wanting to be home with our daughter and guilty for not doing what I believed was needed to prepare for the week ahead.

The financial stress didn't leave just because we had money. If anything, it felt more overwhelming. The stress had shifted from the early days of focusing on providing for our family's needs and paying our employees to fear of losing the wealth we'd amassed and the lifestyle we enjoyed. We were on a merry-go-round moving with centrifugal force, and the only way off was to slam into a concrete wall, which we did, causing a great deal of pain.

After closing the business, we were at a loss as to how to proceed. For ten years, our entire focus had been on building our business, doing whatever it took to meet customers' needs. Kent often reminded me that the greatest cost of doing business is acquiring a new customer, so it was imperative that we kept the ones we had by making them happy, which I enjoyed doing. Furthermore, our customers and employees had become our friends. The business provided a center of gravity around which our entire life revolved.

As the Oklahoma economy continued to collapse, causing banks and businesses to close, the community was awash in painful consequences. Living in Oklahoma felt like we were in a disaster movie. Many of us were in the same boat, but still, our financial woes made us feel like we had a dreaded disease, as we no longer felt we fit within the social world we once enjoyed. Even though others were in similar circumstances, several of our close friends distanced themselves from us, making it seem like they didn't want to risk "catching" the disease of our business failure.

Our attorney advised us to stop making house payments. Given that we were exhausting our limited savings, this made sense—we needed to preserve our capital to buy time to chart the next chapter of our lives. His recommendation went against everything I'd ever learned about being a good person. The daily decisions about what bills and who would get paid were excruciating. I delivered cashier's checks to pay family-owned businesses so they wouldn't get caught in our financial web. Kent and I disagreed about paying our outstanding five-figure tithe we'd pledged to our church. Unfortunately, I won the argument, and we paid it, but I've thought many times how that significant amount of money could have been better used to help our family survive what was to come.

In the meantime, we put our house on the market, but with the economy in the tank, there was no buyer to be found at any price. Our realtor hosted open houses weekend after weekend, and not a single potential buyer came. One evening, when a process-server was pounding on our door—and I do mean pounding—our frightened ten-year-old daughter asked me, "Mommy, can the bank take my dogs away?" I assured her that would never happen.

After about a year, our mortgage lender foreclosed, and we rented a three-thousand-square-foot house in an affluent neighborhood for $500 a month. As the Oklahoma economy was devastated, a bank had foreclosed on the house we were renting and was willing to accept that low rent to have someone living in it, as houses tend to deteriorate when they're not occupied. Meanwhile, our beautiful former home sat empty and our lender continued to drop the asking price in search of a buyer. The irony that we were paying $500 a month to keep our large rented house from sitting empty was not lost on me as I watched our beautiful home sit empty. As per the *New York Times* article, desperation had indeed descended upon Oklahoma.

With the demise of our business, we were now both unemployed, which made the next few years brutally difficult. I cleaned houses to earn enough money to pay our rent and make minimum payments on credit cards to be able to continue to have credit available to buy groceries. Kent struggled to find a way to move forward, with the combined stress of providing for our family, his depleted self-image as a failed business owner, and his sense of guilt and feelings of inadequacy as both a man and a provider. Friends who owned businesses offered him jobs in their companies, but knowing nothing about their industries, he wanted to make something happen in a business he created. He had been an entrepreneur all his life, and that's what he wanted to remain. He tried to use his personal network to put together income-producing projects, but nothing worked.

I was invited to do a consulting project for the accounting department of a property management company, something I could work around my house-cleaning business. In the midst of our efforts to stay afloat, I took classes at a local university to finish the undergraduate degree I'd started my first year out of high school.

As I was working long hours to get good grades, I wondered what I might have accomplished with my life if I'd had an education from a "good school." I looked at the top schools in the *U.S. News and World Report*'s annual college ranking edition. Giving no thought whatsoever to the logistics or cost of attending, or the difficulty of being admitted twenty years out of high school, I called Harvard, Stanford, and Northwestern to get admissions applications. I only completed one application.

I had literally been on my hands and knees cleaning toilets earlier in the day when I stopped by our post office to get the mail from our box. I didn't know that universities send #10 envelopes containing rejection letters and a large envelope with a packet of forms to complete when sending acceptance letters. The envelope from Stanford was not only large, it had the word "Congratulations" written across the outside. As I write this, tears again well up in my eyes. It was the envelope that provided a beginning to a new life, not only for me, but also for our family.

We had a professional estate sale, only keeping what would fit in the U-Haul truck that Kent's brother drove to California for us. Our family of four moved into an eight-hundred-square-foot, three-bedroom married student apartment on campus for four of the best years of our lives. I spent three years finishing my undergraduate degree and stayed an extra year to get my master's degree. Along the way, I lived in Paris for an overseas study program, while Kent took care of the kids for the ten weeks I was gone. We dug a deep hole of credit card and student loan debt, but we were moving toward a better life, and the financial stress was less than what we'd been through in Oklahoma. Kent got a job in sales, but he was miserable working for someone other than himself; again, he tried to cobble together projects to earn enough of a living to augment my student loan income.

After completing my BA and then finishing my master's degree in sociology with a concentration in organizational studies in 1996, a friend asked if I could help her corporate engineering team resolve some organizational conflicts that were keeping them from meeting delivery schedules. That project launched my career in organizational work. Armed with my experience as a business owner and what I learned in obtaining my new degrees, I worked with several early-stage Silicon Valley startup companies that were designing computer chips. Using contacts made with board members of those companies, I worked closely with venture capital firms. For one of them, I was part of the package they provided to help fledgling companies that they funded to launch their new businesses. I was hired typically as the first nonfounding employee to find and furnish office space, open a bank account, set up accounting and human resources systems, and perform the "back office" work for engineering firms.

For many years, I was the steady breadwinner while Kent worked on consulting projects and had various short-term jobs. Eventually, I left the world of startups to build Life Matters Financial Group from a part-time second job to the point where it provided our family income and employed others. In the process, our kids grew up in a home that was tense from the stress of financial hardship, which was made more difficult because they were living in the affluent community of Palo Alto, California. They weren't able to do the same activities or make the same purchases as their friends. I would have been more comfortable moving somewhere more affordable, but Kent enjoyed the intellectual stimulation and entrepreneurial environment of being in the proximity of the Stanford community, and the location provided easy access to the startup companies for whom I worked while doing my client work on weekends and evenings.

These years taught me that Kent and I experienced financial stress quite differently. The most optimistic person I've ever known, he had an enviable way of compartmentalizing his emotions and staying focused only on the things he could do something about. If he felt financial stress throughout those years, it wasn't obvious to me. Because I handled all aspects of our finances, he didn't have the constant stress staring him in the face like I did. He seemed to be comfortable with his ability to ignore what he didn't see, but I found it frustrating.

My coping strategy, on the other hand, was to look the dragon in the mouth on a daily basis. Every day, I opened the bank's website to check our balance and reviewed my Quicken file to see which bills were coming due. This had a calming effect on me that was needed to keep my sanity. I stayed on top of the logistics of paying our bills like a dog with a bone. Even when I could only make minimum payments on credit cards, I paid them the day the statement closed so I could feel a sense of control over the one thing I could control: keeping our great credit. To have endured as much financial hardship as we did and consistently have a credit score in the very-good-to-excellent range took a lot of effort, but it was our great credit score that allowed us access to zero-percent credit card promotional offers that provided the cash flow to get us through some difficult times.

Financial stress was a way of life for me from my earliest childhood memories. Because it was so pervasive, it felt like I couldn't get away from it, like it had a hold over me. Even when we had significant wealth, we paid a high price by working seven days a week to maintain all that we'd accumulated, so the stress never left.

My greatest regret is knowing that we robbed our children of the innocence of their childhoods as they had to watch me obsess about money. I am grateful those days are behind us, which enhances my appreciation for the life I have today. I appreciate that our kids' childhood experiences provided them with knowledge and experiences that have resulted in their wisdom and financial acumen as adults, but it was a helluva price for all of us to pay.

As I retrace these decades of my life—and I will tell you the rest of the story that has brought me to my own healthier, more constructive, and peaceful relationship with money—my hope is that you'll notice components of your own life's trajectory, whether they're similar to or different from mine, to consider how the twists and turns of life have taught you to think about money the way you do. As I've described how my scarcity mentality continued regardless of the abundance of my financial life, I encourage you to reflect on threads of your own thinking that cross all events of your life. I hope my story will encourage you to make a chronology of your financial life to identify thought or behavior patterns behind your beliefs and to discover new ways of thinking about money.

SOMETHING TO THINK ABOUT

- Does my story trigger questions or thoughts in relation to your own views about money? If so, what are they?
- If you're exhausted by your lifestyle, what could you do to reduce the pressure?
- How do you and your significant other experience stress around money? Is it similar or different? How does it affect your relationship?
- What strategies do you and your partner use to cope with financial stress?
- How would a chronology help you discover the source of your thoughts around money?

Chapter 6

Personal Identity Around Money

As I've worked with clients in the context of their finances, I've had an opportunity to be the proverbial fly on the wall, to notice ways that our relationship with money can influence other aspects of our lives. Many of us have not thought about what we think about money or how our thinking permeates our worldview, but we all have a lens through which we see money, and the composition of that lens can determine how we see the world.

As we'll see in the stories that follow, some folks use money to create their personal identities around it, while others need to separate themselves from it. And of course, for still others, money isn't a factor in how they see or present themselves. I invite you to think about how money influences your thinking about who you are and the qualities and values that matter most to you. Again, it's helpful to remember that how we see ourselves in the context of money, whether or not it's a factor in our identity, is neither good nor bad. It just is or isn't, as the case may be. It's likely a pattern we learned at some point in our lives and have held onto without realizing that it has become deeply entrenched. What matters is our awareness of how it influences our self-talk about ourselves as human beings.

Let's take a look at some stories that demonstrate how money can influence our identity.

››› *Gail and Tom*

I was asked to help Gail determine where she stood financially when her husband, Tom, died unexpectedly. In his late thirties, Tom had a classic athletic body and was leading a corporate fitness training class when he died of a heart attack. His tall, lanky frame and lifetime focus on personal fitness made his untimely death even more shocking. Gail was frozen with grief and fear about how she would care for their four young children with the income she earned decorating specialty cakes for a friend who owned a bakery. She was relieved when Tom's brother, Jerry, immediately took on the role of her family's patriarch, making funeral arrangements, identifying an attorney to probate Tom's will, and suggesting that she hire me to provide guidance and support as she sorted through Tom's affairs and planned her family's financial future.

I'd met Gail previously, as I had worked with other members of her close-knit family for several years. To determine how she would move forward, Gail needed to decide if she would continue working while balancing the needs of her children and dealing with her own grief. She thought she might need to find a full-time job and considered how that decision would affect her ability to give her children the attention they needed, especially in light of their father's untimely death. Fortunately, in the process of going through Tom's papers, Jerry found that Tom had a seven-digit life insurance policy through his employer, a policy that Gail had not known existed.

Gail shared with me that she and Tom had struggled financially their entire marriage, not just in terms of available money but even more so over conflicts around how they would spend money. Even when they agreed they could afford things they needed or wanted, they had arguments over the choices each would make, either with individual purchases or when buying things together. As we worked together, Gail told me some of her lifetime issues around money, and I could understand why they caused conflict in her marriage.

Contrary to the more common issue people have with overspending, Gail disliked spending money, even on things she and their family needed. Since their funds were limited, it might seem like her reluctance to spend money would have been helpful; however, the extent to which it caused her pain to buy truly essential items like the kids' clothes or groceries created tension in their household. Furthermore, she had strong opinions about Tom's spending on recreational activities and an expensive hobby, both of which no doubt helped him cope with his job and family obligations.

Perhaps you'll find it surprising that Gail had grown up in a wealthy family. But her father, whom she described as exceedingly frugal, conveyed great pride in her ability to save money as a child. She enjoyed his affirmation and the special attention she got for saving her allowance to such an extent that not spending money became a critical part of her identity. More than once, she told me how her siblings spent all their weekly allowance while she hid her money in a box under her bed. She loved to open the box and count her accumulated wealth more than she enjoyed spending it. After a childhood of reinforcing this sense of accomplishment, coupled with her father's praise, she had difficulty spending money for essential items as she became an adult.

She once told me how proud she was for having spent less than $100 on clothes for herself the year prior to Tom's death. Gail didn't appreciate that Tom enjoyed traveling and recreational activities like bike races or taking weekend family outings to the lake. It didn't help that they didn't have much excess money, and it took the addition of her part-time income to provide enough money to cover the kids' school activities. Between her reluctance to spend and their lack of discretionary money, their choices around spending became a source of conflict in their marriage.

I worked with Gail for several years following Tom's death and observed her situation as it evolved. She put the insurance proceeds in a low-yield bond fund, describing how she would never pay an investment advisor's fees to have her money actively managed. She didn't want her family or friends to know she'd received a life insurance settlement, but of course, Jerry had discovered the policy, so he was aware of her true financial situation. Before finding the policy, Jerry had offered to pay for Tom's funeral and attorney fees to probate the will, thinking those expenses would create further hardship for Gail.

By the time the attorney's statement arrived, she had received the insurance proceeds, but she told the attorney that Jerry would pay his fees based on their initial conversation. In light of the sizable insurance policy Jerry had discovered, and his help processing the paperwork to collect payment, he was no longer willing to cover the expenses that had been incurred as a result of his brother's death. He didn't discuss his change of heart with Gail, so she heard from the attorney's office that Jerry wouldn't pay their bill. The two of them never discussed the payment, which Gail begrudgingly made, resulting in their ongoing estrangement.

From my vantage point, I understood why Jerry changed his mind about paying the expenses after learning of Tom's life insurance policy. He knew Gail had money to pay the attorney without creating a hardship for her family and appreciated how Tom had provided for his family in advance.

Gail talked about her lack of money to anyone who would listen, never mentioning that Tom had left her far more financially comfortable than she'd ever been during their marriage, with significant money to continue providing for her children. She conveyed to friends in her church that she was a "poor widow" who was supporting her young children on her part-time baker's salary. One cold winter night, someone left a package on her front doorstep with new winter coats for her children, the donor apparently assuming she couldn't afford to buy them. Similarly, when she told neighbors that her washing machine had broken, one of them paid for a new one and had it delivered to her.

Gail told her elderly mother that she was working a night shift at a retail store before Christmas to be able to buy gifts for her kids, causing her mother grave concern over her safety being out late at night while the children were home alone. As one who prepared monthly financial reports for Gail, I never saw any evidence of additional income beyond her baker's salary, but for confidentiality reasons, I could not calm her mother's anxiety by revealing the truth. Of course, Gail didn't share this same story with me, as she knew I would know the truth by virtue of my access to her financial records.

Gail also asked friends to host a fundraiser at the high school she and Tom had attended to raise money for her kids' college education, while having most of the insurance proceeds sitting in her bank account. As Jerry had attended school with his brother and future sister-in-law, he commented that he felt like Gail had disparaged Tom by portraying to their mutual friends that Tom hadn't adequately provided for his family. The fundraiser for Gail's children, which Jerry refused to attend, widened the rift between them.

I tell Gail's story not in judgment, but to show how a person's deeply entrenched beliefs about money can become part of their personal identity. Gail presented herself in a disingenuous light to others. As her mother had been a long-time client, she shared with me how she agonized about what would happen to Gail and her grandchildren when Gail reached an age at which she could no longer work. I struggled with knowing the truth, all the while being unable to provide her mother with assurance that Gail likely had enough money to last the rest of her life. Regardless of whether Gail continued working or not, I knew her children's future was financially secure. For confidentiality reasons, I could only listen, saying, "As you know, I can't discuss Gail's finances with you, but I can assure you that she and her children will be okay. I hope you'll share your concerns with her so she can relieve you of any anxiety you're feeling."

››› *Jim and Lois*

In contrast to Gail's identifying herself as lacking financial resources, Jim's story reveals a different relationship with money. Jim was a family business owner who saved for retirement inconsistently throughout his career. As the years progressed and family needs were put ahead of his voluntary retirement savings, the relatively small amount he'd accumulated was not enough to continue the lifestyle to which he and his wife, Lois, were accustomed. Through the years, Jim assumed that the majority of his retirement funds would be generated by proceeds from the sale of his business when he reached retirement age. As it turned out, things didn't go as planned. Economic conditions had taken a downturn, and the business didn't adjust quickly enough to those changes to thrive.

Additionally, Jim hadn't prepared any of his three children to take over the leadership of the company or identified anyone to succeed him as CEO. When a recession started the company on a downward slide just a few years prior to his retirement age, the business couldn't recover. Jim felt lucky to find a buyer who would keep the family name attached to the business, all the while fearing the buyer's intent was to generate a tax write-off they would get by selling assets and slowly gutting the company his father had founded fifty years earlier. In the short term, Jim was able to present the sale of his business to the community as a graceful way to say he retired. However, his retirement savings didn't provide the financial means to continue Jim and Lois's affluent lifestyle. Ultimately, his fears about the new owners closing the business and taking the tax write-off were realized, but at least he was no longer involved with the business. Therefore, most of their friends didn't know what had happened to it or that the family name was associated with a business that had closed.

About five years before he planned to retire, Jim gradually increased his retirement savings and started investing it with a wealth manager. The market had done well enough for it to grow, though he knew it wouldn't be enough to provide for him and Lois if they lived a long life.

By the time Jim was seventy-five, he and Lois had exhausted their available cash and started withdrawing money from their investment portfolio. Knowing he was depleting his investments caused him considerable anxiety, as Social Security was their only income other than a few investment dividends. He struggled with knowing he was not only using the retirement savings but, by dipping into his principal, he was also limiting the ability for his wealth manager to invest money so that it could generate more income. Because he disliked taking distributions from his investment portfolio, he would wait until they had completely exhausted their available funds before contacting his investment advisor, Brian, to ask him to transfer from his investments into his personal checking account.

I started working with Jim to help him take control of his personal finances, as Lois had never participated in discussing their money. Jim was overwhelmed with both the emotional and logistical aspects of everything from paying bills to the complexity of his personal finances. His company's accountant, who had recently died, had handled Jim's family finances for most of his adult life. Even though Jim was an astute businessman—especially regarding high-level financial negotiations—at seventy-five, he had to learn how to do mundane tasks like paying bills and handling personal financial details.

Jim worried that having too much money available in their personal checking account would allow them to spend more than he was comfortable spending. Therefore, I recommended that he establish a reserve account that would automatically get a consistent monthly transfer from his investment account. By analyzing their monthly spending for the previous year, I suggested an amount he was comfortable transferring. This process removed the issue of being reminded how much his investments were being depleted each month while providing available money for unexpected expenses and to pay current bills. More importantly, he didn't have to endure the agony of calling Brian to initiate a transfer when needed. The system helped him feel like he was "on top of his finances," as he called it, and gave him a sense of peace that they weren't using too much of their portfolio for daily living.

Throughout the time we worked together, Jim referred to the money in their investment account as "Brian's money." It seemed to me that his thinking of it as his own money made spending it even more distasteful. Unfortunately, his investments didn't earn enough money to meet their needs for the rest of their lives. It didn't help that Brian had invested a significant portion of the money in high-tech internet stocks, so the crash of the dot-com bubble reduced their portfolio significantly. On October 9, 2002, the NASDAQ-100—which tracked high-tech and dot-com stocks—had dropped 78 percent from its peak, according to Wikipedia's dot-com bubble entry. Their holdings in Enron and WorldCom became completely worthless almost overnight, and his portfolio never recovered from those devastating losses. Ultimately, he sold some personal assets to continue the appearance of wealth that he'd enjoyed while being president of his company.

Jim and Lois were pillars of their community, both serving on influential boards and committees. Shortly before the economic downturn that heralded the demise of the business, they'd built a

> large new home, complete with a garage apartment for a live-in caregiver in the event they would ever need one. The idea of letting their community know the truth about his retirement and the demise of his family business was unbearable, and so Jim lived the final years of his life in fear of the truth being revealed.

Jim's and Gail's stories are quite different, but they both reveal how money can get tangled up with our sense of self. While Gail's sense of identity had been tied to her frugality since childhood and was critical to how she presented herself to the world as an adult, Jim's need to maintain the appearance of wealth also helped create his identity. As the business had grown, so had his stature in the community.

My Story

When I think about my own identity around money, I recall how I felt when our family moved to Palo Alto from Oklahoma City so I could attend Stanford University as a forty-year-old undergraduate. When we left Oklahoma, we hired a professional estate sale company to sell the many household possessions we knew would never fit in any home we could afford in California.

Stanford housing was divided into courtyard communities, each with its own name. These courtyards created mini neighborhoods, as the back of each of the two-story family apartment buildings opened onto a large gated area with picnic tables that provided opportunities for family or community meals, "sand pools" with playground equipment for younger kids, and lots of open lawn for other community activities like volleyball, badminton, soccer, frisbee, and touch football. Our area, Barnes Court, provided some of my fondest memories of holiday meals with friends and neighbors as we moved the picnic tables together to create our Barnes Court family traditions. Being a transient community where students arrived as they started their PhD programs, law school, or MBA programs and left when they graduated, we now have friends around the world whose lives crossed paths with ours during the years we lived there.

Our living in campus housing appeared to happen by accident, though hindsight reveals that it was no accident. Shortly after I accepted Stanford's offer of admission, our family visited Palo Alto the summer before school started. It was obvious that campus housing wouldn't be an acceptable option because of the run-down condition of the apartments and unkempt grounds. As soon as we returned to Oklahoma to prepare to move, Kent returned to California to begin his job search and look for an acceptable place to live. He never returned to Oklahoma, as both affordable housing and a job were more difficult to find than we expected.

After unpacking at our married student apartment, I ventured into the courtyard to meet my new neighbors. As I met them, people often asked why I was there. I was an anomaly because of my age, the fact that I was an undergraduate student living in graduate student housing, and I was the only resident with a teenaged daughter. After a couple of days of repeating my story, I was exhausted. I noticed how often I'd told new acquaintances about having owned a business and leaving a large house.

I'd felt the need to convey that the standard of living in this shared student-housing apartment complex wasn't what I considered acceptable. Of course, I had no idea where others had come from or what their standard of living might have been, but it felt like I was shouting from the rooftops to anyone who would listen that it certainly wasn't mine. After a couple of days, I realized I was likely conveying a message others didn't want to hear and, in the process, was embarrassing myself. Consequently, I no longer felt compelled to reveal the details of my former life.

Just as Gail and Jim used money to provide evidence of their place in the world, I'd done the same thing. When nobody knew anything about me, I used the size of our previous home and business ownership as shorthand to say, "I am a person of substance. I was important in my community." I cringe as I reflect on those early conversations, with the hope that the listeners have long since forgotten the extent to which I revealed my insecurity.

I grew up hearing the phrase, "Keep up with the Joneses," which meant having material possessions that conveyed relative wealth. It was used pejoratively, as a way to describe people who bought demonstrably expensive items that friends and neighbors might have thought they couldn't afford. Money is often used as a measuring stick, both by others to determine where we fit in relation to themselves, and also to help us identify for ourselves how we think we fit in our communities. We all have perceptions of what it means to have money, to save money, to spend money, and to have enough money to invest. We might want to think about how we incorporate these ideas to create our identity, as well as how we see others.

SOMETHING TO THINK ABOUT

- How do you present yourself when it comes to your finances as you interface with your friends and community?
- What, if anything, do you want others to know about your financial status?
- What information would you be uncomfortable disclosing to others about your financial situation or past?
- As you reflect on the stories in this chapter, what aspects of your life or observations about others' lives come to mind?
- Which, if any, of your material possessions do you want to convey a message to others about your financial situation?
- What possessions do you use to determine your opinion of others' financial situations?

Chapter 7

How We Make Financial Decisions

As you reflect on your thoughts and beliefs about money, you might find it helpful to consider processes you use to make financial decisions. Let's consider some factors that influence your choices and how these might differ depending on the nature of the decision at hand.

Do you make financial decisions as easily and in the same way that you make other decisions? For example, do you find decisions around money difficult in ways that others aren't? Is it easier to make emotional decisions or those related to ethical or moral questions? What about creative, artistic, spiritual, or religious decisions? Might this be an indication that you could better understand why your emotions are different when money is involved? Consider the following:

- Do you approach decisions from a place of abundance or scarcity?

- Are you clear on your own ideas about what these terms mean to you?
- Is abundance having enough (however you define "enough"), or is it having more than you need or could ever use or want?
- Is your scarcity or abundance perspective the same for both financial and nonfinancial issues?

Perhaps you feel like you demonstrate an attitude of abundance in some cases and scarcity in others. If you buy a lot of things, do you think that indicates an attitude of abundance? For example, it could be that you think the act of purchasing is evidence that you have confidence in your monetary resources (or credit card limits) to make these purchases and have your needs met. You might even be energized by thinking that being able to make these purchases reinforces your sense of well-being.

On the other hand, maybe you make purchases not from a center of abundance mentality, but more from a place of scarcity, using what's sometimes called "retail therapy" to calm your anxiety or soothe an aching heart. Or maybe to reassure yourself that you matter, you buy to remind yourself that you deserve what you've bought.

It might seem counterintuitive to think you shop to overcome feelings of scarcity. I'm reminded of the title of Geneen Roth's book *The Craggy Hole in My Heart and the Cat Who Fixed It*. Maybe you have a craggy hole in your heart for which you're seeking relief, and you shop to try to fix it. Regardless of how many times you try and fail to gain relief, you continue to seek it through shopping. Evidence that relief can't be found in owning yet another cashmere sweater—regardless of how good it might feel against your skin—is of no consequence when you've developed a pattern of shopping to fill the craggy hole in your heart. This is why the term "shopaholic" correctly describes the practice—it operates like an addictive pattern.

Some fascinating research shows how entire industries work to seduce us to spend our money in mind-boggling ways. For example, in the Netflix documentary *Minimalism*, author Joshua Becker says that we see five thousand advertisements a day that all tell us, "This is what your life should be about: accumulating more things or focusing on you." Juliet Schor, PhD, economist and sociology professor at Boston College, describes how we tend to think of fashion as something to throw away, not when clothes are no longer usable, but when they no longer have social value or are no longer considered fashionable. And Rick Hanson, PhD and neuropsychologist, says, "You can never get enough of what you don't really want. Deep down, we don't really want more goodies, more toys, more cars; we want what they will bring us. We want to feel whole; we want to feel content." We want to fill the craggy hole in our hearts.

Does this conversation make your heart beat faster or give you an uncomfortable sensation? If so, you might want to notice what you're feeling and where in your body. For now, keep in mind that we're opening doors to understanding. Let the light shine on the darkness that you might be feeling but haven't yet identified. Remember, we're sitting on the curb having a conversation, and I'm asking you to tell me about it: Sweetheart, what's making you cry?

Do you have differing emotions around purchasing, depending on the cost? When we feel something is at stake if we make a "bad" decision, we can feel fear or resistance to making the decision. I recall a friend telling me how she felt sick to her stomach when signing the mortgage documents to buy their new home. She described how her hand trembled as she signed the papers and how she thought about all the unforeseeable ways their commitment could go wrong.

As someone who had stopped working professionally in the early days of their marriage, she felt dependent upon her husband to provide their sole income. To think of making the house payment if ever she had to earn enough money to pay it herself caused her significant angst, especially since their new house payment was three times that of their previous home. Today, more than thirty years later, their mortgage is paid in full, and she laughs about the anxiety she experienced in her late twenties, as she and her husband entertain their grandchildren in that same house.

Another friend struggles with buying cars, whether new or used. He wants to get the best deal possible, and the effort he puts into negotiating is fraught with anxiety that he might "leave money on the table." Even though the process of buying cars has changed significantly with the introduction of the internet and car-buying apps, he holds on to the old way of going to a dealership and negotiating with a sales-person, who then requests approval from a sales manager. Many times, my friend has left a dealership without buying a car after spending hours negotiating to get the "deal" he wants but can't get. He's needed a new car for several years now and has spent several days shopping for one, but he continues to leave the dealership without buying. He's rented a car for day trips during this time because he's not confident in the reliability of his now twenty-three-year-old car.

He doesn't struggle with other purchases in a similar way. I once asked why he thinks that might be, and he told me some family stories about how his dad struggled with each new car purchase, typically complaining that the dealership had gotten the "better end of the deal," that the car didn't fit their family's needs like he'd thought it would, or that he didn't like certain things about it—another example of how we hold onto our parents' patterns.

It's helpful to identify our typical process of making financial decisions and think about why we do what we do. Perhaps we notice that we regularly follow a set pattern in the process we use, and then realize that we have a habit of throwing our process out the window under some circumstances. Why do we create arbitrary rules for spending our own money, and then, under different circumstances, change the rules or disregard them completely?

Have you thought about how differently you feel when making spending decisions, depending on the item you're buying? I think the answers as to why we do this are as varied as the number of people reading this, but I can tell you that we all do it—and rarely do we think about what we've done or why, until our credit card statement knocks us for a loop or a decision creates conflict with our partner.

It's not uncommon to have certain amounts in mind that we're comfortable paying for a purchase, but the amount we're willing to pay can be wildly different depending on the item. For example, my daughter Heather tells me she'll pay $3.99 to rent an iTunes movie, but she won't pay $5.99. She laughs as she tells me she has no idea how she arrived at those amounts to create her rules for herself. In contrast, when she was checking in for a flight from Nairobi to San Francisco, an offer for an upgrade to business class for $1,000 per person appeared on her computer screen. The same woman who won't pay $5.99 to rent a movie hesitated only briefly before jumping at the chance to spend $2,000 in upgrade fees for herself and her daughter, Amina, to fly business class.

As she and Amina had lived in Nairobi for several years, they made many long flights in coach seats. Amina had asked to fly business class since long before the age when most kids would know the difference. Heather had great fun surprising Amina as she handed her a boarding pass that said "Business" when they were about to board their flight. Nine-year-old Amina's initial response was to question her mother's wisdom in spending the money to fly business class, which provides a wonderful example of the age at which kids have already started developing ideas around money.

I understand my daughter's splurge for the upgrade for herself and Amina. I find that regardless of how much money I have, whenever I'm buying something for Amina, I have no hesitation about spending whatever the item costs. Even when money was scarce, I never felt the tightening in my chest when I was buying for Amina, even though I agonized over spending money on myself. I didn't give a second thought to spending money on a frilly ballerina dress that she didn't need and would quickly outgrow—but hopefully would love wearing. How much fun it was to buy it and send it to her in Nairobi, paying nearly twice as much for the shipping as I'd paid for the dress! One time, I bought her some clothes, books, and toys. When I took the stack of items to FedEx, which was the only way to get items to her in Kenya, the shipping was going to cost more than $300. As I hadn't spent anywhere close to that amount on the items, that was more than I was willing to spend to get them to her. I stood at the FedEx counter, asking the clerk to tell me the revised shipping cost as the weight changed when I removed items, starting with the heavier ones. Finally, when the cost was down to about $125, I stopped removing items and paid the shipping cost. I justify paying shipping costs to Nairobi by remembering that it's the cost of having a grandchild who lives overseas, and it's important that she gets little gifts from Grammy.

I see other adults making similar choices around spending money for their children and grandchildren, or another special little someone in their lives. Or, maybe someone who is not so little. As in my example, when we're buying for our kids or grandkids, we often use a different set of self-imposed rules, with wildly different emotional responses from those we might have if we were spending the same amount of money on someone else, or even ourselves.

I've noticed that for clients who tend to take pride in being frugal, special-numbered birthdays or anniversaries often have different rules. Whereas they might typically spend $50 on birthday gifts, maybe they'll spend $500 for a twenty-first birthday gift for a son, daughter, or grandchild. The same is true for anniversaries, when a couple will spend extravagantly for a twenty-fifth or fiftieth anniversary trip when they typically have a nice dinner to celebrate other years.

More important than the amount spent is how we feel when we create a story to tell ourselves about the amount we've spent. Maybe we justify the cost to ourselves or try to make sense of why we'd spend this amount on this particular item. Or maybe we feel the need to explain it to our partner. I don't say this pejoratively, as it's our money and we can spend it however we want. It's simply something to notice as we think about the unwritten rules we establish for ourselves and the lengths we go to in order to justify changing them, based on what we're buying or for whom.

Additionally, as we live more and more in a cashless society, numerous research studies show that people will spend twice as much for the same item if they're paying for it with a credit card rather than cash. If you'd like to better understand why this phenomenon occurs, I encourage you to Google "spending cash vs. credit cards," and you'll see about sixty-nine million results.

With the advent of Apple Pay, Venmo, PayPal, Zelle, and other apps that let us easily transfer money between friends and family, the lack of need to carry cash is so great that my young clients—from the youngest at age twelve—hardly know what to do with it. They tend to see it as a nuisance. Research suggests that paying with credit cards disconnects the emotional impact of a purchase from its cost, due to the delay in payment. This detachment can lead consumers not only to spend more money but to be less aware of the cost as they make purchases. I'm curious how the current generation of teens might struggle with using value as a guiding factor when making purchasing decisions.

I'll go into more detail about it later, but the first argument of my marriage about money started with my husband asking how much of my own money I had spent on clothes for myself on a shopping trip. Sometimes our partners think they have a right to an opinion about how much we spend, and on the specific items we choose. In my case, I made it clear that I worked to earn my money, and I didn't intend to have my purchasing decisions questioned in the future. In fifty years of marriage, we've never had another argument about the amount of money either of us has spent. As Kent had watched his parents' interactions around items his mother bought and his dad questioned, he understandably followed their pattern. When I pushed back with a different idea of how we would interact around money as a couple, that was all it took for him to never question my purchasing choices again.

Another area that elicits different emotional responses around money is travel. When we lived in Oklahoma, we tried to go to New York City at least three times a year for long weekends. We enjoyed going to Broadway plays and other cultural venues. We had our favorite fine restaurants and stayed at the Plaza Hotel (in its heyday, before most of the rooms were converted to condominiums). We typically stayed only three or four nights because we couldn't afford to stay longer in terms of time or money. We would often see three Broadway plays during our short stay, visit several museums, and of course, shop at stores we only heard the names of in Oklahoma City—like Saks Fifth Avenue, Bergdorf Goodman, and Godiva Chocolates—before their stores became ubiquitous across the country. I would add that I don't typically like to shop, but the electricity in the air in New York City charges my batteries in ways that make me feel like I am in a fairy tale.

It was as if we were traveling and wouldn't be there long, so we threw caution to the wind and had a wonderful time, feeling freedom to spend more money than we'd ever spend at home without giving it a second thought—until the credit card statement arrived the following month. The excitement and joy of the moments in New York had dissipated by then, and the staggering credit card balance provided an "Oh, shit" moment. We had the money to spend, so it wasn't as if paying the credit card bill presented a hardship. It was just that we'd never have spent that much money if we'd been at home, and seeing the total amount felt so different from the excitement we'd experienced when ordering whatever we wanted on expensive menus and paying scalper rates to see Dustin Hoffman in *Death of a Salesman*.

Similarly, the first time we went to Hawaii on a business vacation, we stayed at the luxurious Mauna Kea Resort Hotel, which at the time was a Rockefeller resort. Being in beautiful surroundings, while having every need graciously met by hotel staff, we went to the hotel jewelry store and bought a string of coral beads as a memento of our visit. Those beads probably cost several times more than they would have if we'd bought the same ones in a jewelry store at home. I haven't worn them more than a couple of times through the years, as I never had clothes they would accent. And yet, in the spur of the moment, we spent several hundred dollars that we'd never have spent under any other circumstances on something I've hardly ever used.

I'm typically not one to buy something I'll rarely use. Now, when I see the necklace at the back of my jewelry box, I have a moment of self-flagellation because I think about the unnecessary waste of money, despite easily affording it. Apparently, it served a purpose, because I haven't made another impulsive purchase of the same magnitude since.

››› *The Carter Family*

> In contrast to our way of traveling, the Carter family used a different strategy. They decided how much they would spend in advance of their trip so their spending wouldn't create stress or anxiety. As they planned a three-week family vacation to South Africa, Barry made a financial plan that included a lot of approximations, but nonetheless, the results accomplished exactly what he wanted. He did a significant amount of internet research to determine a ballpark amount that their family of four would need to spend daily for food and lodging. He included the cost of airfare and car rental, as they would spend most of the three weeks driving around the country from Johannesburg to coastal towns on the Indian Ocean.

After they returned home and the final tally for their trip was calculated from the credit card statements and cash receipts they'd saved, they were delighted to learn they'd spent about $500 less than Barry had projected. Whereas on past vacations buyer's remorse had landed like a brick when credit card statements arrived, the Carters discovered that this time they felt good about the amount they had spent and could focus on the wonderful memories they'd created. Spending a bit less than Barry predicted gave them a sense of accomplishment and a strategy they would use whenever they planned future vacations.

Beyond thinking about how we make decisions for what could probably be called "special circumstances," let's look at some of the processes we frequently use. Please keep in mind that we're being flies on a wall, seeing how different people make their decisions. We're not judging them or comparing ourselves to others, thinking, *Well, I'm not* that *bad*. We're simply noticing how we might see their experiences as a way to think about our own ideas and habits. As I've watched people—from the extremes of self-identified shopaholics to those who find it painful to spend their money—I've come to understand that the process for making financial decisions is as varied as the people who make them.

››› *Frankie*

My friend Frankie had several years of sobriety. Unfortunately, she replaced addiction to substances with an addiction to shopping. She discovered she couldn't walk through a store without buying something she hadn't previously wanted, which led to buying something else to go with what she'd just bought. Thousands of dollars later, by the time she arrived home laden with shopping bags, she usually felt a serious case of buyer's remorse. Therefore, she made herself a rule that she wouldn't—or as she described it, "couldn't"—trust herself to go inside a retail store to shop.

Shortly thereafter, she went to Neiman Marcus to return an expensive pair of boots she knew she'd never wear, commenting that she really didn't know why she'd bought them, because she didn't even like them. On her way from the customer service desk where she returned the boots, she noticed a dress hanging on a mannequin and left with more than a thousand dollars' worth of new clothes, spending far more than the boots had cost.

After this incident, she tried shopping online to avoid the allure of stores, but that soon became problematic. She knew that her "witching hour" for online shopping was after dinner, when her favorite TV programs hadn't yet begun and she had nothing to occupy her time. She would pick up a magazine and see something she liked, and it would become a challenge to find that very item online. She was invigorated by the hunt, describing the experience as providing the high she had previously gotten from substances. As she visited the websites of her favorite stores, she would find items that were similar to whatever she'd seen in the magazine and put them in online carts, all the while continuing to look for the exact item. Along the way, she often lost track of what she'd put in carts and placed multiple orders for identical items from different stores. Then she would search for accessories to go with the original item. With their large home, she had the luxury of ample storage, including entire closets for specific items like purses or shoes.

By the time her purchases came in the mail, she often couldn't remember having ordered them. Then she'd have self-chastising thoughts, which led her to do more "retail therapy" to relieve her self-inflicted pain. It was a financially unsustainable, emotionally debilitating cycle. Often, she'd ask me to return a backseat full of items to local stores from which she'd ordered online, so she could avoid going inside.

My heart hurt for her as she struggled, knowing her money was limited—and when it was gone, she would have no means by which to earn more. Even more heartbreaking, she only left her home to buy groceries and attend twelve step meetings, as she identified herself as agoraphobic. She had few places to wear the beautiful clothes, shoes, and accessories she loved to buy.

As we discussed her spending habits, she described how the thrill of the chase to find what she'd seen in magazines drove her decisions. The fun was in the getting rather than in the having. When she hired a professional closet organizer to help purge her crowded closets, she donated more than thirty ten-gallon trash bags full of clothes, many with price tags still hanging from them.

At the opposite end of the spectrum are people who find it painful to spend money, especially on themselves. I first observed this in two different college students with whom I worked.

››› *Sam*

Interesting, but not surprising, is that one who didn't like to spend money was Sam, the son of Frankie. Having grown up watching his mom's piles of packages arrive on their doorstep, Sam went from being extremely frugal during college to cautiously wise after graduating and being self-sufficient, living in a different town from his mom. As we planned his college spending together for each upcoming semester—so his trustee could transfer the money that would be needed to cover his tuition, housing, books, and ancillary expenses—he identified and quantified each type of expense, carefully making sure he wasn't drawing more from his trust than he'd need. His trustee didn't care what the amount was but said he would make only one bank transfer each semester. Sam made his decisions based on his own internal desire to spend only what he considered to be necessary. By the time he graduated, he had enough left in the education trust that his grandparents had left him to provide a down payment on his first house.

One might wonder why Sam's and Frankie's ways of making financial decisions are so different. Where does Sam's internal governance come from? We can imagine how he might have felt as a child watching the struggles his mom endured. He watched the turmoil she experienced as she moved from highs to lows as the excitement of getting things shifted to the stress of paying for them.

I can't possibly know the extent to which Sam consciously decided to make decisions about spending that were significantly different from his mom's, but as we've worked together, he has become acutely aware of his own beliefs and the reasons behind them. Having worked with him for over a decade, I appreciate how he shares his thinking as he makes financial decisions, always with prudence and wisdom. As a result, he has a quality of life around finances that he enjoys and can easily maintain.

››› *Heidi*

For another college student, Heidi, spending money on herself was so painful that she would eat only the two meals per day that were covered under her dorm meal plan. Even though her parents paid for her education, she worked through the work-study program in the dining hall and got a second part-time job in a doctor's office. As she didn't have a car to drive off-campus, she took a city bus to get to the doctor's office, which further ate into the time she had available to study and do intramural sports that she enjoyed. Since her expenses were covered and her parents sent money for incidentals, she had no need to work. Still, she chose not to use the money her parents sent, saving it instead.

Heidi's parents appreciated her helpful attitude and desire to work but didn't understand what drove it. Her mom described how difficult it was to hear her daughter talk of anxiety over her limited time and money, especially when she didn't understand why Heidi felt the need to work. Because a relationship with money is deeply personal, it's difficult to understand how others think about theirs. As I've watched Heidi grow into adulthood, she has continued to be cautious with money. She keeps her sizable bank balance in a savings account where it earns little interest because the risk of losing it by investing it is too frightening. While she is exceedingly responsible with her money, it creates significant stress. She says thinking about money is painful for her.

Donna

Similar to Heidi, Donna had significant anxiety around money, though her anxiety came from watching her brokerage account rise and fall. She had invested a sizable divorce settlement in the stock market. Having stayed home for years to see her children through school, after the divorce, she took hours of training to become a life coach—and her business thrived. Her income supplemented her earnings on her invested settlement but would never generate the kind of money she needed to maintain the lifestyle to which she was accustomed. Therefore, the thought of losing her investments in the market created so much fear that she checked

> her online balances daily, watching as the value rose and fell. After several years working with various types of investment advisors, she moved her money into a money market fund with low returns, but she was relieved to not ever have to watch the balance plummet. She valued her peace of mind over potential gains in the market.

Through the years, I've observed many clients as they tried different strategies to curtail their spending. As we've seen in Frankie's case, she noticed that she went online to shop at a particular time of day. You might notice other factors around your spending. If this is something you struggle with, I encourage you to try different strategies to see what works best for you. Here are a few that friends and colleagues have used:

- Keep cash in bags in the freezer and thaw only what you intend to spend when you go shopping.
- Have a written plan when going shopping and buy only what's on your list.
- Especially for large purchases, create a holding period of twenty-four hours to three days between the time you find the item and make the purchase, to see if you really want to buy it.
- When dining in restaurants, drink water.
- Leave your credit card at home and shop only with cash.
- Don't let yourself get allured by bargain sales.

This list is by no means exhaustive. You might want to Google "strategies to stop spending" to get twenty three million more ideas about what might work best for you.

In addition to these types of issues, I've noticed how different living situations change spending habits, simply by being alone or with someone else. I find that people often make financial decisions differently when they're made on one's own versus those that are made as part of a couple.

››› *Harold, Helen, and Joanie*

To give an example, I started working with Harold and Helen Taylor when they sought my guidance in making use of their limited retirement income. Harold had made some unfortunate investment decisions that he felt shame around, having lost substantial amounts of money. He had a lifetime monthly pension check and did occasional consulting work that generated additional income, but Helen worked as a travel agent to augment their monthly income. Her salary not only provided them with additional income but, more importantly, gave them opportunities for low-cost exotic travel, where she led tours. They hired me to help them get a better sense of what they described as "how we're doing." They told me that money had been an ongoing source of conflict in their long marriage. Tragically, about a year after we started working together, Helen died unexpectedly.

Harold was devastated and struggled to get through each day. As we met weekly after Helen's death for me to administer her estate, I was concerned about his well-being. He spent significant money on his adult children and grandchildren and tried to use his retirement funds to make more money by investing in several shady schemes that a "friend" coerced him into. Harold's son eventually told the friend not to call his dad again. Harold always saw good in people, even when others saw evidence that people didn't have his best interests at heart. He had difficulty saying no. He donated significant sums he couldn't afford to organizations when asked to serve pro bono on their boards, always with an expectation of a significant financial contribution from him. He was a pillar in the community, with a generous heart and inordinate knowledge about a myriad of diverse subjects, so his involvement was a tremendous asset to these organizations. Still, he had little appreciation for the value of his intrinsic contributions, so he contributed money he needed for his own financial well-being. Between the money he lost in unscrupulous investments and donating more than he could afford, his finances were a constant source of anxiety.

One day Harold got a phone call that changed his life. He was asked to move to another state to take a year-long interim position as the head of an organization until a full-time replacement could be hired. Within days, things fell into place, and he was able to rent his furnished home for more than twice the amount of his house payment. Simultaneously, a friend, Rick, who lived in the town where he was going, called to tell Harold that he was having some changes in his life and would soon be moving. As they talked about what was happening in their lives, they realized that Harold could rent Rick's home for the year he'd be living there. Harold's transition into his new life went well, and he enjoyed living in Rick's home. His work provided a sense of belonging, something that was especially meaningful after Helen's death.

One Saturday, Harold noticed a garage sale in his new neighborhood and stopped to see if there might be any items he could use. Knowing Harold as I do, I'm sure he was more interested in having the opportunity to meet his neighbors than in finding items to buy. As he looked through the items on a table, he chatted with Joanie, whose husband's recent death after a long illness had prompted the garage sale. Harold picked out a few items and said his goodbyes, but on the walk home, he was surprised to find himself thinking about Joanie in a way he hadn't thought about a woman since Helen's death. He looked for other opportunities to see Joanie in the neighborhood, taking walks that passed her house in hopes of bumping into her. He asked her to join him for lunch one day, and after declining his invitations several times, she finally agreed.

As she tells the story, she wasn't interested in having lunch with a man so soon after her husband's death, but Harold wore her down, and she agreed to go to lunch to stop his asking. As she seemed to know everyone in the restaurant, Harold discovered that she was well-known in the community. Noticing that Harold seemed to enjoy being with people, it wasn't long before she invited him to join her at community events. Even though she was recently widowed, their relationship progressed rapidly, possibly faster than it might have otherwise since Harold's year-long assignment was coming to an end. When it was time for him to leave, rather than flying home, he

> and Joanie made the three-day road trip in her car, thinking that she'd stay with him a few weeks and then visit her adult children, who lived nearby. As so often happens, the universe had other plans, and after a few months, they were married.
>
> Joanie and Harold had significantly different ideas about taking financial risks and, more importantly, whom to trust with their money. As happy newlyweds, Harold typically went along with whatever Joanie wanted to do. Harold had developed a pattern of using money while he was widowed to fill the craggy hole in his heart. When Joanie entered the picture, they merged their finances. She had a pension from her deceased husband, along with some income from her parents' estate. She quickly put a stop to Harold's practice of giving large charitable donations and providing money to his adult children, as he'd been doing since Helen's death. She began managing their finances, a task he was delighted to relinquish. Today they live a financially stress-free life, meeting their daily living needs, remodeling and furnishing their home, and taking wonderful trips, all without the conflict or anxiety Harold had grown used to.

Sometimes we are aware that we are making decisions about financial matters that we know aren't cost-effective, even as we're making them. I'm reminded of four different clients who made similar decisions around their home mortgages. Even though they had low-interest-rate mortgages with a cost-saving tax deduction for the interest paid, they each chose to pay their mortgage balance in full, using invested money that was earning a significantly higher rate of return than the low rate of their mortgages. Without exception, they each said a version of, "I know it doesn't make sense financially, but I have peace of mind knowing my home is debt-free. It is mine and nobody can take it away from me." For these clients, this was a financial decision they made knowing why they made it, and I fully supported their choice to put peace of mind over financial considerations.

I find it interesting that in all four of these situations, the person making the decision thought they needed to justify to me that they knew it wasn't the best financial decision. They seemed to think I had a preconceived idea that they should always make the most financially effective decision. Please know that you never need to justify to anyone why you make the decisions you do, especially ones that put your peace of mind over financial cost.

As we've seen in these stories, a lot of factors lie just under the surface of how we make financial decisions, many of which we are unaware of unless we are open to exploring why we do what we do with our money. If you find yourself wanting to change your relationship with money, it will be helpful to recognize the patterns you use. Pay attention to your feelings as you use different strategies to make financial decisions. You might want to think about the various reasons you buy certain items, the circumstances around your purchases, and your feelings after buying them. For example:

- Do you experience buyer's remorse, and under what circumstances?
- If you find that you make impulse purchases, like my coral necklace, is there a pattern to when and where you tend to do this?

- Do you find that you shop to give yourself a reward or to alleviate depression or longing for someone or something other than what you've just purchased?

Your discovery likely will put you on the path of understanding what you can do differently to enhance your relationship with your money.

SOMETHING TO THINK ABOUT

- As you think about your way of making financial decisions, do you think it's similar to or different from the way you make decisions that aren't financial? What are the differences, and why?
- As you read the stories in this chapter, did you find yourself thinking how you might have reacted similarly or differently in these situations?
- Do you have a "craggy hole in your heart" that you're trying to fill? If so, how do your strategies help or not?
- Do you have areas of your life where money doesn't guide your decisions, i.e., buying gifts for certain people or special occasions, traveling, or when other factors are considered? What are they?
- If you've ever made a financial decision where you thought, *I know this doesn't make good financial sense*, how do you think about that decision today?
- Can you identify some of your self-imposed rules around money? Do you know where they came from? Do they serve you well?
- If you look at your spending over a long time-horizon, do you see changes that occurred because you were either single or in a relationship?
- Would you benefit from creating some new self-imposed rules around your money, and if so, what would they be?

Chapter 8

Gender Income Inequality

Issues around money can result from factors beyond our control. Nonetheless, they impact our lives and often our relationships. While we have no control over the macroeconomics of the society we inhabit, we do have control over our conscious awareness of those factors and how we internalize, react to, and respond to them. For example, issues around income disparity cross race, social class, age, and gender in the United States. We also have drastic inequality in household income between the top-earning 20 percent of households and those in the remaining income quintiles, as well as differences in earning potential, particularly across race and gender differences. For our discussion, we'll focus on the disparity in earning potential across genders and the ways it sometimes manifests as conflict in meaningful relationships. This is not intended to ignore or discount the importance of other aspects of income inequality, but to focus on the one I hear most often from clients as a source of conflict, and with which I, as a Caucasian, third-age woman, have personal experience.

We'll look at three significant issues around women's income that cause problems in relationships: (1) equal pay for equal work, (2) women earning more than their husbands or partners, and (3) husbands who don't work.

Are you familiar with Equal Pay Day? This might be called an American holiday for women, as it is designated annually, but certainly not one to be celebrated. It identifies the calendar day on which women in the same professions have earned the same amount of pay that their male counterparts earned in the previous calendar year. For example, in 2025, women worked until March 25 to earn the same salary men in their same professions had earned by the end of 2024. Care.com's 2018 study revealed that, across 525 professions, women worked 66 days more than men to earn the same salary. As financial managers, women worked an additional 154 days to match the annual salaries of their male counterparts.[1] On average, women earned 20 percent less than men in the same professions. And these data don't begin to address the many ways this disparity impacts society, such as women's access to health care, nutrition for themselves and their children, educational opportunities, career advancement, and their ability to provide for their families. The underlying message is that women's time, effort, experience, expertise, and credentials are not valued as highly as those of men.

The disparity in income between genders for the same work has an even greater effect when the woman is the sole breadwinner, especially as a single mom or as part of a couple where the partner doesn't work. The additional time she must work to earn the same income her male partner could earn doing the same job is time taken away from her family and herself. If a man had the same job, he would earn more money in less time, allowing him to spend the additional time however he chooses.

Pew Research found a significant shift in earnings for husbands and wives—from 1972, when 5 percent of wives were primary breadwinners and 11 percent of married couples had equal earnings, to 2023, when 45 percent of couples earned equal amounts or wives earned more than husbands.[2] Still, numerous studies and reports find that the consequences to individuals and relationships when women earn more vary, from greater substance abuse for men, to feelings of resentment for both partners, tension and instability in the marriage, increased likelihood of divorce, higher stress and feelings of inadequacy among men, and feelings of guilt among women for emasculating their husbands.

Let's look at some stories that move our understanding from macroeconomics to reveal the personal impact of these issues.

My Story

During my first marriage (the one that started when I was eighteen and ended at twenty-one), I asked for a raise that was in line with the added responsibilities of my evolving job. My boss, Stan, told me he couldn't give me a raise—which he acknowledged I deserved—because, as he stated, "Your husband's ego can't handle you making more money than he does." Stan had been a personal friend of our family for more than half my life. He had attended my wedding and knew my situation better than other bosses typically would. Still, he had no right to assess how his granting my request to be adequately compensated might impact my marriage.

Ultimately, Stan's comment proved valuable, as his observation made me aware of issues that led me to see gaping holes in my marriage—issues that ultimately led to divorce.

In fact, his observation clarified my resolve not to let my husband hold me back from accomplishing what I wanted. Even though Stan's response to my request for a raise had a good outcome, the way it happened was so very wrong. His comment was sexist, misogynistic, patriarchal, and inappropriate. Today, it would be illegal. If asked, he would have said he was trying to protect me, as he would his own daughter, but even that explanation was a distorted assumption that I needed protection because I am a woman.

While we're talking about Stan, I would be remiss not to mention that he sent me, his twenty-year-old secretary, to pick up a sizable check from an important customer. As the man, old enough to be my father, handed me the check, he leaned over and kissed me on the lips. I was so shocked that I didn't know what to do. As I had the check in hand, I turned away and ran to my car. By the time I returned to the office, I was sobbing so much that I could hardly explain what had happened. As I told Stan and his wife, who was co-owner of their business, about the kiss, Stan assured me that he would "make Bill pay for what he's done." Later, "when the opportunity presented itself," as Stan told it, he seemed proud of his "resolution": increasing Bill's price for our product to "make him pay for what he did." As prices were fluid with every shipment of our product, Bill could not have known why the price was increased without an accompanying explanation, which Stan did not provide. Stan was clueless but thought he had taken action to make Bill pay. Of course, his method of retaliation did nothing to address my feelings or Bill's behavior.

Tala and Kyle

I'm reminded of another marriage that ended in irreconcilable differences, in large part because of the wife's higher income. Tala describes how earning more than her husband became a significant factor in their divorce. Married at twenty-three, she thought she and Kyle were "on the same page," as she describes it, in most areas of their lives. A couple of years after they married, as they were discussing the amount they could afford to spend on their first house, Tala realized how different their aspirations were, how little Kyle was willing to work to have a successful career, how their work ethics diverged, and how far apart their financial goals were. She shared with me that they didn't have a similar drive that would lead to comparable life trajectories.

When Kyle described to Tala's mother—in a tone she interpreted as jealousy—that Tala would always succeed in ways he never would, her mother began to see evidence of cracks in their marriage. She revealed this conversation to Tala, as well as other observations that caused her to see the handwriting on the wall, only after their divorce.

More than the disparity in income, the difference in their attitudes toward work troubled Tala most. She felt like she was pulling more than her share of the weight in their relationship, including earning power and hours devoted to work. She began to lose respect for Kyle, due to what she described as his "lack of ambition." Their once similar interests that had brought them together now revealed the extent to which they were going in different directions.

As she reflected on ways her feelings had changed over the course of their marriage, she considered the questions she wished she'd asked herself before committing to a long-term relationship: Were there signs of his lack of ambition? Did he exhibit the jealousy when they were dating that her mother later perceived? Had they been on the same page during their courtship, or had she only seen what she wanted to see? Why hadn't they discussed their long-term aspirations, which might have revealed the looming differences that would prove fatal to their marriage?

Besides the disparity Tala experienced with Kyle at home, things were not going well at the investment brokerage firm where she worked. She noticed that no women attained the level of director in her office. She described how she and her female colleagues were doing work that made their bosses—the directors—look good, but they had neither the title nor the salary to compensate them for their efforts, which their bosses took credit for. When Tala discussed that she was doing the work of a director and asked to be recognized and compensated accordingly, her boss didn't deny she deserved it but told her they didn't have a budget that year to consider her for a director position. Ultimately, Tala concluded that no woman would be allowed to advance in the company, so she became the fourth woman in her department to leave.

As Tala was a highly respected employee, the day she tendered her resignation, the CEO of the company asked to see her. As he professed surprise that she was leaving, he asked her what he could do to change her mind. She replied that it was too late and took advantage of the opportunity to share her observations with him. He was dismayed to hear this news, saying he was not aware that women weren't being promoted in their company. After her departure, Tala stayed in touch with some of her former colleagues and was informed that women continued to be passed over for promotion.

When Tala discussed with her brother, a university professor, how Kyle didn't share her passion for work, he commented that he'd noticed a difference between the efforts exhibited by men and women over the ten years he'd been teaching. He voiced concern for the generation of men that had come through his classes in recent years. He observed that women tended to exhibit a greater passion for learning, a drive to excel academically, and career aspirations they actively pursued. In contrast, his male students seemed less interested in the coursework and less motivated to attain academic excellence.

Apparently, his observations map to national data; *Psychology Today* reported in 2018 in a review of three hundred studies involving more than one million participants from around the globe that girls have been getting better grades than boys for decades. Girls not only do markedly better in language classes, but they also outperform boys in math and science. (The female advantage in school performance in math and science does not typically appear until the adolescent years.)[3]

From my viewpoint, the ways in which women's income inequality has been "justified" have changed little through the years. Tala was told within the past five years that she could have neither the salary nor the title of director because of "budget constraints," but in the context of a company with no women directors, it was obvious that this explanation was code for "women not allowed" at this level of management.

In earlier times, and not that long ago, women were told they made less than men doing the same job because "men have families to feed." My mom was given this explanation when she asked for a raise at a major oil company, where she worked in the accounting department. Of course, she also had a family to feed, and no child support to help make ends meet. In that era, her boss didn't need to use "budget constraints" as an excuse, like Tala's boss. It was acceptable to reveal that a woman would not be allowed to earn as much as a man—and even justified in a way that would not be legal today. (This practice continued a generation later. A friend of mine, who worked as part of a two-income family of four in the 1970s, was told she couldn't make as much as a man she supervised, for exactly the same reason.) To add further insult to injury, my mom's supervisor also told her she needed to slow down the pace of her work because her male coworkers couldn't keep up with her productivity. He actually told her she was "making the men look bad."

When our business became successful in the 1980s, Kent and I planned to divide our salaries evenly between us, as I was truly an equal partner in all aspects of the business. When we discussed our intentions with our CPA, he advised us not to split our income equally because the IRS would likely consider my salary to be "too high for a woman." He indicated that the IRS might consider a significant portion of my salary to be dividends, which would be taxed at a higher rate than ordinary income at that time, and furthermore, the business would lose the tax deduction of my salary expense if that happened. Given that possibility, I begrudgingly agreed to take 35 percent of the total we'd allocated, while Kent got 65 percent. Today, I would not agree to this division, but times were different then. As a woman who has experienced income disparity my entire life, the injustice feels overwhelming. Even after all these years, recounting this story makes me angry.

››› *Professor Dornbush*

As I think about financial inequality, I'm reminded of a situation that results from differences in socioeconomic status rather than gender. A lecture in one of my Stanford sociology classes touched me deeply because it reminded me of my mom, who never earned an annual salary of more than $3,600 (that's not a typo). To impress upon his students the difference in life situations resulting from socioeconomic status, Professor Dornbush described how a middle-class woman on her way to have lunch with friends might experience a flat tire as an inconvenience. She likely would call AAA to change the tire and be late for, or might even have to miss, the luncheon. He contrasted her situation with that of a single mom with four kids, driving to the first job interview she'd had in months, who also had a flat tire. She had no AAA membership, possibly didn't have a spare tire, had no money to buy a new one if needed, and the consequences of missing the job interview could mean that she wouldn't get another chance to earn a living for

> her family, possibly for several more months or forever. This resonated with me deeply because, as a child, I experienced similar situations. I saw the anxiety that car trouble caused as I watched my mom's reaction to a flat tire, fallen muffler, or stalled engine, knowing she didn't have the money to resolve the problem. It was a frightening and hopeless feeling.

Yet another issue that you might find surprising is that it's not uncommon for women to be the sole breadwinners in families that look like any other family with two working adults in the home. In 2016, the Brookings Institution reported that seven million American men between the ages of twenty-five and fifty-four were neither working nor seeking employment, representing about 12 percent of men in their prime working years.[4] From my experience with clients, I see that spouses, children, and often extended family members seem to be ensconced in efforts to cover up the fact that the man does not work.

I'm not describing families with stay-at-home dads who have made a choice to be the caregiving parent or pursue artistic endeavors like writing or visual arts. Instead, in several families with whom I've worked, both husbands and wives seem to go to great lengths to keep the outside world from knowing the husband/father doesn't earn an income.

I wonder why spouses and children seem to think it's advantageous to hide from their friends, and sometimes from extended family, that the husband/father doesn't contribute financially to the household. And I wonder why I've heard comments suggesting that our society considers women being "forced to work" because their husbands don't, whereas I've never heard the phrase "forced to work" used to refer to a man who is the sole breadwinner.

I've worked with a number of families where a man in his forties, fifties, or even sixties has earned little or no income throughout most of his adult life. In all these cases, the men are intelligent, physically capable, typically well-educated—sometimes with postgraduate degrees—and caring, loving husbands and fathers who are deeply involved with their families, but they do not work to earn an income. When talking to their partners, I hear comments like, "He *wants* to work. He talks often about getting a job, but he can't bring himself to look for one," or "I don't understand why he won't get a job." I've noticed that as more time passes without working, the thought of going to an interview seems to become more frightening and less likely to happen. The men seem to feel bad about themselves for not contributing financially, while their partners shoulder the financial responsibility alone. It seems that they are reluctant to participate in their communities, and I've wondered if that's a result of their fear of having to talk about what they do professionally. As the question "What do you do?" is often a starting place for getting to know someone new, their way of avoiding the question is to avoid places where they'll be asked.

In my clientele in Silicon Valley, several of these men are entrepreneurs but don't have income because they either don't have a current project or they are working in a startup where venture capitalists who are courted to invest in their businesses expect founders to work for some time without pay while a product is being proven. I've worked in a number of these startup companies where the founders worked for years without pay before getting funded. When they received their initial funding, the venture capitalists didn't let them repay the years of lost income but instead recognized founders' "sweat equity" in the valuation of the business. In the meantime, the wives or partners of the founders provided for their families, often building a significant amount of resentment.

As we've seen, the situations vary greatly in these stories, but the ramifications can be far-reaching across multiple facets of society. When women earn more than their husbands or partners, they often feel guilty and are more likely to get divorced. When they aren't compensated fairly for the work they do, they're given insulting excuses as to why it's acceptable for them to receive less than men for the same work.

This disparity has extensive consequences for our society, beyond divorce rates. While other women may have different emotions around it, I personally find that it creates resentment, frustration, disdain for patriarchy, and a sense of powerlessness and injustice. These emotions require energy that would be better spent focusing on positive endeavors that enhance our world. As we've seen how the stress of income inequality and out-earning partners can lead to conflict and divorce, we do well to remember the benefits of women identifying and discussing our feelings with our significant others. Even when conversations are difficult and painful, the consequences of not having them are likely to be even more so.

SOMETHING TO THINK ABOUT

- What are your experiences with income inequality?
- If you're a man, do you think about income inequality?
- How has income inequality impacted your relationships?
- Do any of the stories in this chapter resonate with you? How are they similar to or different from your experiences?
- What evidence have you seen that gender income inequality has had an effect on your personal life?
- If you and your partner have significant differences in income, do you discuss how you feel about it? Why or why not?
- Have you ever discussed with your parents or grandparents how income inequality impacted their lives?

Chapter 9

Ways We Earn Money

Does it matter *how* we earn our money? Or even *that* we earn money? Does it only matter that we *have* money, regardless of how we got it? Do people with trust funds who don't need to work for income choose to work for other reasons? Let's talk about how earning money has changed over time and explore various ways people earn their living and the ways their choices are perceived and rewarded.

Recently, I've been thinking about artistic creativity and its meaningful impact on the quality of our lives, as well as how it relates to money. Obviously, some people use creativity in their paid jobs, while others use it as a recreational outlet. Some have a hybrid relationship with creativity that allows them to earn money to augment their steady income, while others use it for pure enjoyment. A graphically creative friend once told me that she wouldn't be able to enjoy making her creations if she were paid for what she makes, and that knowing a customer was awaiting delivery would take the fun out of her inspiration to create. Therefore, she struggles financially to make ends meet, but even her financial needs aren't enough to motivate her to use her artistic talents to earn money.

Some people work to develop their creative skills more intentionally than others, and some are more naturally inclined toward what we typically think of as "creative" work. When we use the term, we're often thinking about artistic expression in the form of a tangible product like a painting, fabric art, music, book, photography, video, or movie. The list is endless. But creativity is also expressed in home decorating, architecture, landscaping, environmental design, packaging design, developing a business plan—and this list, too, is endless. Some types of creativity lend themselves to being compensated more highly than others.

A great deal of effort is often put into guiding children toward careers where they'll be able to "make a good living." Chase Jarvis, founder of CreativeLive and author of *Creative Calling*, conjectures, "The human brain evolved to keep us safe, not happy—it will resist your efforts to walk your own path because creativity challenges certainty."[1] I would add the word "security" to "certainty." As society seeks certainty to keep its children safe, parents are charged with the responsibility of raising children who are contributing members of society and have the skills to provide for themselves and their families. Unfortunately, the meaning of "contributing" can become problematic when financial value is assigned to how we, as their children, want to spend our lives. Our parents are often more concerned with the amount of money our choices will enable us to earn than with trusting that we know what will bring us joy, contentment, and satisfaction. They might do well to remember that even with the possibility of climbing a career ladder, most jobs have limitations as to the maximum amount they'll pay, so few careers provide limitless financial opportunities.

In the US, lawyers and STEM careers (e.g., engineers, financial wizards, investment advisors, scientists, surgeons, computer hardware designers, and software developers) tend to be more highly compensated than those that require fewer technical skills. Therefore—obviously with some exceptions for those who have achieved critical acclaim—teachers, musicians, singers, artists, actors, architects, landscape designers, authors, inventors, storytellers, and interior designers tend to be paid less. However, Daniel Pink concludes in *A Whole New Mind* that many technical jobs can be automated or outsourced to countries that pay far lower salaries than those in the United States. And he projects that more creative tasks like package design and marketing will become more highly valued, to the extent Pink says they will "rule this century" and consequently command higher financial compensation. I know some people might be thinking, *From Pink's words to God's ears!* Unfortunately, until the shift that Pink predicts occurs, those who want to pursue their passions in more creative careers will likely be limited as to how much they can earn.

Furthermore, the days of having, or even wanting, a single career in a lifetime are gone. Baby boomers, who were raised in homes with typically a working father whose goal in life was to retire with a gold watch after a lifetime with the same company, often followed in their parents' footsteps. They thought their children would follow their path, staying in a career that their education or first job led them toward. Some of them have difficulty understanding that the uncertainty generated from the lack of job security creates opportunities for their kids to live more satisfying lives. According to a CNBC article published in February 2021:

> Younger Americans are updating some of the tactics in career switches for a changing world. Not only are younger workers seeking job mobility, but they're also looking for flexible and remote work schedules, a need that came to the forefront amid Covid-19. Many younger workers are also incorporating skills training to market themselves as more competitive candidates.[2]

Let's take a deeper look at how the work world has changed.

››› *William*

My friend's dad, William, is an example of how careers used to be. He was honored at his retirement party with a grandfather clock after working for Mobil Oil for fifty years. As the company later became ExxonMobil, as we know it today, we see how it has evolved, and I doubt that many of its current employees would have been there long enough to have twenty-five-year careers, let alone William's fifty years. Its employees have evolved too.

To consider how drastically the workforce has shifted just in my lifetime: In 2015, the Bureau of Labor Statistics reported that the average worker held ten different jobs before age forty.[3] This is in contrast to the pressure that parents of my generation used to help their children make one "right" career choice. As we've seen with ideas about money being carried forward from our ancestors, expectations around career choices are too. How many families have created dynasties within a particular profession, particularly legal and medical ones, that children know they're expected to continue?

Contrary to how older parents might have guided their children, we now see examples that remind us there's no longer one way to launch a single career that safely puts us on a trajectory toward a lifetime of satisfaction, happiness, or financial security. And if someone thinks they can tell you how to live your life, I beg you not to consider income as *the* deciding factor in your choices. Let's look at some stories to help us think about factors that impact how we have come to the decisions that set us on our life paths.

››› *Elle*

Author and artist Elle Luna, in *Your Story Is Your Power: Free Your Feminine Voice*, tells of coming from a long line of attorneys.[4] Even when she was living as an artist, skipping meals so she could make art, she applied to nine law schools. Believing she could not pursue creativity as her livelihood, she assumed she needed to go to law school. When her application was rejected by every single one, she describes feeling like a failure. Only then did she see that her desire to go to law school stemmed from the messages she'd internalized about what was valued in her family. Fortunately for the readers of her books, Elle realized that she had the freedom to "make better choices," as she describes it.

››› *Abby*

My friend Abby did attend law school, but by her second year realized that being an attorney would never be a fulfilling career for her. She was far happier helping friends organize their closets on weekends than studying law. As a kid, she organized drawers and closets throughout her childhood home, including those of her three siblings. She left law school to follow her passion and has built a thriving estate sale and organizing business in the San Francisco Bay Area, employing more than a dozen people and providing an invaluable service to her appreciative clients.

››› *My Father-in-Law*

I'm reminded that a song by a street fair singer-songwriter affected me so profoundly that I still recall the words decades after watching his performance. Perhaps living in Silicon Valley made the lyrics even more poignant, as they describe the nature of engineers I worked with in high-tech startup companies. The song tells of a young man who wanted to spend his life following his passion of writing songs, playing his guitar, and performing, but his dad wanted him to be an engineer. The words also touched me deeply because I'd watched as my father-in-law lived his life as a businessman, despite coming home from being a medic in WWII thinking he'd found his calling to be a doctor. While he was in India during the war, his father bought a business for them to run together, and he obediently followed his dad's plan upon his return. I have no doubt that, while his business skills provided a good life for his family, following his heart would have made him a truly special doctor.

››› *Philip Glass*

Composer Philip Glass drove a taxi and worked as a plumber to earn a living while writing operas, even while he was gaining notoriety writing music that is heard round the world. He tells the story of installing a dishwasher in the home of a customer in 2011:

> While working, I suddenly heard a noise and looked up to find Robert Hughes, the art critic of *Time* magazine, staring at me in disbelief. "But you're Philip Glass! What are you doing here?" It was obvious that I was installing his dishwasher and I told him I would soon be finished. "But you are an artist," he protested. I explained that I was an artist but that I was sometimes a plumber as well and that he should go away and let me finish.[5]

››› *Heather and Her Roommate*

Our daughter Heather, at the age of twenty-six, attended a job fair for international schools in San Francisco. Both she and her same-aged roommate were offered positions teaching in other countries.

> Heather had offers from three countries, while her roommate's offer came from Tokyo. When Heather called to say she was leaning toward accepting an offer from the Democratic Republic of Congo, I told her, "You go, girl!" When her roommate called her parents, they told her she couldn't go—that Tokyo was too far from home.
>
> I've often wondered about the path her roommate's life took, if she continued to let her parents dictate her choices. I think about my own difficulty in knowing my career path. Therefore, I wouldn't tell my kids, or anyone else, how to walk theirs. It's hard enough to determine which twists and turns to take without having someone else think they know what's best for us. And yet, many young people are faced with the dilemma of following their hearts or listening to ideas their parents project onto them in an effort to lovingly protect them.

Another consideration when deciding how we want to spend our lives is the cost of earning a college degree. As government-backed student loan debt has reached crisis proportions of $1.6 trillion in the United States, we'd be wise to consider the value and benefits of a college degree in relation to the cost of getting one. After graduation, borrowers are often limited in their ability to contribute to the economy, as their loan payments can keep them from being able to buy their first home, purchase a reliable car, or start their family. Debt repayment creates a stranglehold on many young adults—an obligation they feel like they'll never be able to repay. The burden is so heavy that many people have ignored their federal student loans until they reach the age when they're ready to draw Social Security.

As of 2025, about 1.3 million Social Security beneficiaries have federal student loan debt, with approximately 35 percent being in default, which means they are at risk of having their benefits reduced.[6] The share of consumers aged sixty and older with outstanding student loan debt quadrupled from 2005 to 2015, to 2.8 million from about 700,000 people, according to a 2017 report from the Consumer Financial Protection Bureau.[7] When I was consolidating nearly $200,000 in student loans for myself and the parent loans I held for both of our kids, I was asked how long I wanted the repayment period to be. I asked what would happen if I died, and I was told (though I don't think this is true any longer) that the loans would be forgiven. Since I'd gone to college at the age of forty and was consolidating at fifty, I told the woman to make them thirty-year loans, as I'd be eighty by the time they were paid off. I was willing to bet I'd die before I paid them in full. Fortunately, I was able to repay them much sooner than I expected, but I understand firsthand the stranglehold of student loan debt.

Given the enormous societal cost of student loans, as well as the repayment cost to those who borrow the money, some people are now questioning the belief that a college degree is a required path for most students. Many industries have developed training programs specific to their corporate needs. Examples include Google's "Google Career Certificates," which offer a selection of professional courses that teach students foundational skills to find employment[8]; Cisco's Networking Academy, which offers training and certification programs; and other training programs from Microsoft, Apple, and other tech companies. The practice of company-specific training crosses many industries, from biotechnology to business analytics to life insurance to retail and beyond.

Additionally, according to a Yahoo! Finance press release: "Enrollment in vocational and trade schools is seeing record growth, with numbers almost doubling between 1999 and 2016, according to the National Center for Education Statistics."[9] Beyond specific careers with big-name companies that provide training, there's a reason for the growth in vocational and trade schools. When our sewers back up or our air conditioning breaks in hundred-degree weather, we suddenly assign greater value to those who do plumbing and HVAC repairs, even while complaining about their rates for a service call.

What is it about the collective psyche of Americans that assigns changing values to work efforts, depending on our immediate personal needs? When children describe their parents' jobs, at what age does judgment seep in to the perceptions of their classmates? Why does this happen? How does it influence our career choices or our choices about which university to attend?

Having lived for thirty years in Palo Alto, California, home to Stanford University, where 80 percent of residents have at least a bachelor's degree and 92 percent of high school graduates attend college[10], I can attest to the pressure placed on children to get a college degree. A nationally publicized cluster of teen suicides began while our son was in high school. Palo Alto has four times the national average of teen suicides[11] and is considered a "suicide cluster" by the CDC, with its investigation finding that between 2010 and 2014, an average of twenty children per year died by suicide in Santa Clara County, where Palo Alto is located.[12]

As part of a parent group for our son's cohort that met weekly from the time our kids were in sixth grade through their freshman year of college, I heard the anxiety parents felt around which university their children would attend—never around whether their child would attend college or take another path toward adulthood. As college admission letters were received their senior year, one parent explained how her son didn't want to attend Harvard, but her husband told him that since he'd gotten in, he was going. Other parents seemed saddened by their child's opportunities, based on the colleges where they were offered admission. One mother was reported by her child to be so distraught when he didn't get an acceptance letter from Stanford, she closed herself in her bedroom for a week, sobbing at the "knowledge" that her son couldn't be successful without a Stanford degree.

This pressure from parents around the schools their kids attend seems to be driven by several factors. Loving parents at our meetings often described their dream that a few universities would give their child the greatest opportunity for success in life, which usually translated to earning copious amounts of money. They didn't discuss the way their child would fit into the university's culture or cope with the rigors of its academic demands. I never heard one of them discuss how some kids dream of livelihoods that may never create significant earning potential.

))) *Trevor*

I'm reminded of Trevor, the owner of a car body repair shop, who thrilled my soul when he returned my little red sports car to its original condition after I had a minor accident. As we discussed his family-owned business, he described how his Stanford teaching credential and love of working with students weren't enough to keep him in the high school classroom, where he'd taught auto shop for ten years. He needed more income than a teacher's salary could pay to provide adequately for his family, so he turned his weekend hobby of tinkering with cars into a full-time business. Having grown up in Palo Alto, his parents had encouraged him to apply to Stanford, as they didn't consider a lifetime spent working on cars to be a worthwhile career path. And so he did what so many kids do; he followed the path his parents wanted for him. When he made the decision to leave teaching at one of the top high schools in the state, he felt like the weight of the world had been lifted from his shoulders. Not only is he doing work he loves, he's also making more money than he could ever have made teaching, even in Palo Alto.

I will never understand how, as a society, we claim to value education and have data that tells us that a more educated population is better for the entire country yet remain content with paying teachers at the bottom of pay scales that require a college degree. While some states pay better than others, even those at the upper end do not compensate teachers adequately for the important work they do or the skills required to do their jobs well. As parents discovered during Covid-19 school closures, the task of teaching is far more difficult than many could have imagined. Jokes have been told about the lengths to which parents would go to keep from having to teach their children at home, after learning what it took during the pandemic. Yet as time has passed, it doesn't seem like parents have been willing to pay higher taxes or make other accommodations so that teachers are paid salaries more commensurate with their value.

SOMETHING TO THINK ABOUT

- Are you following a career path that you truly want?
- When thinking about your quality of life, what factors besides money do you consider?
- What messages do you want to give your kids about careers they might consider pursuing?
- What would you do differently around your career and earning money, given the chance to do it over?
- How would you feel if your kids wanted to attend trade school or pursue an alternative to college?
- How have your experiences informed your thinking about the importance of a college education?
- How have student loans—for yourself, your partner, or your kids—impacted your life?

Chapter 10

Needs vs. Wants

Blessing #26: May You See Less As More
How much is too much, and how little is too little? The concept of needs vs wants has become muddled in a society that suffers from material and sensory overabundance. Paradoxically, the less we wish to hold on to, the more peace wishes to hold on to us. Thus giving up what we don't need is a liberating act and a spiritual practice. It has the power to simplify, bring in discipline, and align us with our higher selves. The emptier a room, the more space there is for us to walk and admire everything we have. But how do we know when it's enough? It's simple. *When we have enough to be grateful for, when we have time to relish what we have, we have enough.* (italics mine)

—Ashima Sarin, *108 Blessings*

For some of us, anxiety over having enough money is driven by the difference in our understanding between needs and wants. Most of us feel stressed when we don't believe our needs will be met. But the rub lies in understanding the difference between "needs" and "wants" for each of us. Some might feel they have enough if their basic survival needs are met. Others might say their needs would have to be *comfortably* met not to feel stressed about money. For still others, feeling like we have enough might require that both our needs and wants are satisfied.

For our purposes, let's agree that we're talking about needs beyond those essential to living a life free from worry about food and shelter. Therefore, we'll agree to define needs as something for which we have a deep yearning, often something that we're willing to make significant sacrifices to obtain. Thinking about needs and wants, I love this quote by Epicurus, the Greek philosopher: "Remember that what you now have was once among the things you only hoped for."[1]

We do well to remember that one person's "need" is often another person's "want" and understand that both are artifacts of our life experiences. The messages we got as kids around items considered "basic" shaped our sense of security. For example, some families believe they *need* a summer vacation that provides family togetherness, fun, relaxation, and good memories. For others, a summer vacation might be an unaffordable dream, something so far out of the realm of possibility as to never be given a moment's consideration. As a kid, I didn't know I was missing family vacations because neither my family nor my friends' families took them.

Trevor Noah, in his memoir *Born a Crime*, tells of eating caterpillars when he was a kid to stay alive in his home country, South Africa. He describes how his mother ate mud patties. Having been to several countries in Africa, I'm reminded of how our American concept of basic needs varies greatly from that of people in many other countries.

How money is viewed in different countries is as varied as

the people who live there. I've experienced daily life in seven African countries. In Kinshasa, I saw cassava plants—used for food—growing in a tiny triangle of dirt in the median of a four-lane road. As I watched a woman pick a handful of leaves, my daughter explained that cassava is grown anywhere a patch of dirt exists, as many dwellers have no land to grow crops. Similarly, Micae Martinet describes in *Growing Soles: A Memoir* how she witnessed food growing in tiny patches of soil in the middle of roads as she walked across China. These experiences have given me a sense of profound appreciation for my good fortune of being born in America, where food is grown in garden plots or fields, whereas roadway medians hold flowers that enrich our lives.

I'm awestruck by the joy I've seen on the faces of Africans as they walk miles each way to and from work. I'm reminded of how we Americans often think we need "stuff" to make us happy, when the extremely poor people I've seen in South Africa, Kenya, the Democratic Republic of Congo, Uganda, Zambia, Swaziland, and Lesotho have joy in their lives that doesn't come from the brand of clothes they wear, homes with running water, or dining in restaurants. I don't mean to say that American poverty can be discounted. Way too many children in America go to bed hungry and don't get adequate nourishment to thrive. But I would be surprised to learn that those children eat caterpillars for days on end or that their mothers grow their food on road medians.

In contrast to these experiences, I'm reminded of an incident I still remember from forty years ago. Kent, Heather, and I went to McDonald's for lunch. Heather was about five at the time. That particular day, the credit card machine wasn't working, and the counter attendant told us after we'd ordered that they could only accept cash for payment. The total price was about $25, and we had only $20. Not having enough to pay for what we'd ordered, we started taking items off the trays, one at a time, until we had enough cash to pay for what remained. As we ate lunch, we laughed at the experience, noticing that the one thing we weren't willing to remove was Heather's Happy Meal. As we thought about what we'd done, we realized we could have gotten her a hamburger and shared some fries for much less than the cost of the Happy Meal. She could easily have done without the toy and whatever else was in the Happy Meal. And yet, we acted as if we thought removing it would be depriving our child, which we didn't consider to be an option. Her Happy Meal quickly became a "need," while everything we'd ordered was a "want."

When I was about ten years old, I wanted a new bicycle more than anything in the world. I'd gotten hand-me-down boys' bicycles from my older brother as he outgrew them, and I desperately wanted a brand-spanking-new girls' bicycle. Many years later, I remember both the feeling of wanting that bicycle and the thrill of getting it. I earned the money to buy it by doing chores at home and clipping grass between chain-link fences for neighbors. For months, I scanned the Sears Roebuck catalog, drooling over the picture of the blue bike I envisioned as my own. I knew the price by heart, and with each addition to my money drawer, I tracked the remaining amount I would need to get my bike. I vividly remember the day I finally had enough: the layout of the Sears store as I found the bike section, making the purchase, and riding my new bike to my friend's house when I got home. And mostly, I remember the joy as I rode it for many years to come. It was the first time I'd earned money to get something I wanted.

Was my bike a need or a want? At a practical level, it was a want, but for it to have carried so much weight in my memory so many years later, I'd argue that, at that time in my life, it was a need. For most American kids, a new bicycle is easily a want. But to have wanted it so badly—to have known my mom didn't have the money to buy it for me, to have worked till I had blisters on my hands from clipping grass, to have counted my money every week for the many months it took to save enough, and to have experienced sheer joy at owning and riding it—that blue bicycle evolved into a psychological need. And the lessons I learned in the dreaming, planning, acquiring, and enjoyment of it have served me for a lifetime.

Sometimes, the determinant of whether something is a need or a want depends on the circumstances. Our daughter, Heather, has lived in four countries on the African continent over the past eighteen years. Our granddaughter, Amina, was born in South Africa, and they currently live in Nairobi, Kenya. When I received a text from Heather saying they were coming to the United States for the first time since Amina was born, I was shopping at HomeGoods in the Bay Area. I sat down on the pavement outside the store and cried tears of joy at the news. Being separated for long periods of time is a way of life I keep on my mental back burner. Most of the time, being together is a "want" I can compartmentalize. However, when I knew I had a specific arrival date to anticipate, my want became a need to hold them in my arms.

Does it matter if something is a need or a want? As with many things in life, the answer is: It depends. Especially when money is scarce and difficult choices must be made, the distinction becomes mightily important. A problem often occurs in couples when one person sees something as a need and the other as a want. Sometimes, like with my blue bicycle, we want something so badly that getting it might begin to feel like something beyond a need, more like an obsession.

The distinction between a need and a want can matter when we're in a relationship, especially where spending joint funds might prevent the other person from having what they want or need. Perhaps our partner doesn't understand the depth of our desire for a particular object or experience. Sometimes, other issues underlie our actions. For example, if our partner provides the only income in our family, maybe—without realizing it—we give them the power to decide how money will be spent.

Perhaps it's not an item but an experience we want desperately. If you've ever been separated for long periods of time from someone you love, you may know the overwhelming desire to be in the presence of that person. Perhaps your partner or child is deployed in the military or goes away for an extended time for work, school, or travel. Perhaps you live in different cities or on opposite coasts, and the distance feels unbearable. How we feel emotionally about the money it costs to be together can become a significant component in our decision to spend it.

››› *Doug, Emma, and Susan*

> Sometimes our needs don't carry a similar significance for our partner. Doug and Emma's casual conversation turned into a heated argument when she mentioned how she'd been thinking about wanting to see her best friend. Susan had moved to Montana the year before, and Emma missed their daily walks to Starbucks. Many mornings, they chatted over lattes and pastries until lunchtime. The more Emma talked about Susan, the more she yearned to see her, to put her arms around her, to have one of their legendary Starbucks chats. Doug was half-listening to Emma one evening as he thought about his weekend plans with friends.

As Emma talked, she was surprised when tears filled her eyes. She hadn't realized how much she needed to see Susan. Doug appeared to be irritated with Emma's crying.

"You and Susan text all the time," he said. "Why are you crying?"

"I miss her so much. Texting is not the same as being together."

As she defended her feelings, Emma yearned to be with Susan even more.

Doug upped the ante with, "You know we can't afford a trip right now."

"That's just your excuse because you don't want me to go. You spend money on fishing trips with your buddies," she replied.

"I need those trips to wind down from work," he argued.

Emma knew that Doug was right about their not having money for her trip, but still, she huffed defiantly, "You don't think my relationship with Susan is important enough to justify the expense. Well, it matters to me, and I'm going to see her."

With that pronouncement, Emma left the room, slamming the door behind her. The tension between them dissipated as they went about their day. As Emma thought about what had happened, she realized that she really needed to see Susan. What had started as a casual awareness of how much she missed her friend ended up creating a pit in her stomach of loss and loneliness. She resolved to get her needs met, knowing she needed to lower the temperature in the room with Doug. After dinner, when they'd both settled down, Emma told

> Doug that she often experienced his attitude as being dismissive and uncaring. He said he hadn't understood how much Emma missed her friend and that he'd be willing to forgo a fishing trip so she could go to Montana.

Again, we see how money becomes a component in an argument that has far deeper roots than the financial ones. Money can be a convenient tool to avoid discussing underlying issues in a relationship that will continue to surface until they're resolved. Letting money be the temporary scapegoat rarely, if ever, serves a good purpose.

We also see how choices about where we live can take on more than just a desire to live in a particular place. When our family moved from Oklahoma City, which had the lowest per capita housing cost in the nation at the time, to Palo Alto, California, which had one of the highest housing costs, I became acutely aware of the impact of cost of living on choices we make about where we live. If asked, I would have said we couldn't afford to move, but when it became a necessity that enabled my education, cost wasn't an issue. Until we moved to California, I had no understanding of the extent to which the cost of living in Oklahoma went far beyond money. I never questioned that I would likely live my entire life in Oklahoma. My lifelong friends and family were there. It had always been my home. Because housing costs were so low, homes didn't build enough equity to be able to move to other parts of the country. When a friend returned to Oklahoma after moving to Atlanta, she told me, "Until I got out of here, I didn't understand how different life can be." Her comment resonated enough that I remember her saying it, but until I experienced life elsewhere, I didn't grasp the magnitude of her statement.

Even after living in Palo Alto for nearly thirty years, I still marveled at the deep blue sky, the ability to have flowers blooming in my garden year-round, and the lack of wind, thunderstorms, and tornadoes I endured during the first forty years of my life in Oklahoma. I don't think the beauty of the Bay Area will ever get old. As I now live on Kaua'i, "the Garden Isle," where there are no words to describe how the beauty of nature, the proximity to the ocean, and the nourishing bounty of the island feed my soul, I can't imagine a scenario that could make me leave, and it has nothing to do with financial cost.

››› *Jimi*

My Facebook friend Jimi recently posted that she longs to live in her "happy place," Colorado, but she's lived for decades in another state. She says her husband of many decades is a terrific guy, but "his one flaw is that he won't live in any other state" than where they live. Jimi writes that she's "forced to live in a place that feels like being imprisoned." As she replies to one of her friends, "There's something a bit heartbreaking knowing we have this one life to live and can't be where we need to be. Not want, but need." To which I say, "Exactly!"

››› *Karla*

A lifelong friend, Karla, who lives in a landlocked state, recently told me that she needs to live near water. As we discussed her upcoming visit to Kaua'i,

> she talked about how she could never afford to live in Hawaii. I encouraged her to think differently about her situation, not to see her desire from a perspective of cost, but to consider the joy she believes living near the ocean would bring her. Every time she talks about wanting to live near the ocean, her husband replies, "Let's go!" I asked her how often they use the three bedrooms and formal living and dining rooms in their large home, and whether she might be willing to live in a smaller house in order to fulfill their dream of living near the ocean. She replied that she's not ready to leave a lifetime of friends and family, so obviously, cost is not the only thing keeping her from living elsewhere. When we know what we need to feed our soul, I would argue that, even though we might not know how, we *can* find a way to make it happen. We need to be clear about what is driving our choices, and it's easy to blame money.

Where we live matters. Our environment matters. Of course, we make our decisions about where to live for a myriad of reasons, but when we know our heart as clearly as Jimi knows her desire to live in Colorado is "not want, but need," or as deeply as Karla believes she was destined to live near the ocean, then the reasons we give ourselves for not following our hearts' desires could use some further examination.

To leave you with a final thought on the consequences of needs vs. wants: Our perception of the terminology really matters. Or, put another way, ensuring that our passions are honored matters a great deal. Being able to determine if an item or experience is a nice-to-have want or something about which we care deeply enough to be a need can help us spend our limited resources of time and money to have the things that provide joy and meaning in our lives. When you know what's worth fighting for, the phrase "pick your battles" takes on important meaning.

SOMETHING TO THINK ABOUT

- What items or experiences in your life are needs for you but wants for other people who are important in your life?
- How does conflict between needs and wants get played out in your significant relationships?
- Does your partner spend money on items that you would never buy? If so, how do their choices affect you?
- If you don't live in a place that feeds your soul, would you consider moving? If not, what's stopping you? How might you overcome this hurdle?
- Having read this chapter, what do you want to discuss with your partner about your needs and wants?
- Is there something you know is a need, yet you don't have it? If so, can you find a way to attain it that you haven't previously considered?

Chapter 11

How Much Is Enough?

Before we discuss the issues in this chapter, let's remember that it reflects American experiences, while millions of people around the world don't have the luxury of considering these topics.

A sense of not having enough can have many origins but often includes angst around money, whether it comes from childhood experiences or our current financial situation. Nobody can decide for you how much is enough or what it would mean for each of us to have enough. I often hear women encouraging other women, saying, "You are enough," which makes me wonder: Why are women comforted by the reassurance that we are enough and other women know we appreciate being reassured? The conversation is a reflection of receiving and internalizing the opposite message—that we may *not be enough*. When we don't feel like we're enough or we don't have enough, we typically operate from a sense of scarcity or constant depletion.

While reasons abound for a sense of not being enough, much of the blame has to be laid at the doorstep of industries that relentlessly tell women we aren't enough. Worse, they tell us if we spend enough money on their products, they can make us into what we can't otherwise accomplish. We discussed in Chapter Seven how different industries try to seduce us out of our money, but in my opinion, the multi-billion-dollar beauty industry does some of the worst harm to women's self-esteem. Just take a look at book titles about the ways the beauty business affects us:

- *Made Up: How the Beauty Industry Manipulates Consumers, Preys on Women's Insecurities, and Promotes Unattainable Beauty Standards*, by Martha Laham
- *All Made Up: The Power and Pitfalls of Beauty Culture, from Cleopatra to Kim Kardashian*, by Rae Nudson
- *Made Up: A True Story of Beauty Culture Under Late Capitalism*, by Daphné B. and Alex Manley

Just these few titles alone tell much of the story of the industry. Martha Laham's book description on Amazon goes further:

> *Made Up: How the Beauty Industry Manipulates Consumers, Preys on Women's Insecurities, and Promotes Unattainable Beauty Standards* is a thorough examination of innovative, and often controversial, advertising practices used by beauty companies to persuade consumers, mainly women, to buy discretionary goods like cosmetics and scents. These approaches are clearly working: the average American woman

will spend around $300,000 on facial products alone during her lifetime.

A friend whose business organizes closets, drawers, and cabinets for clients often posts before-and-after pictures of projects on her website. The volume of drawers upon drawers and cabinets upon cabinets of beauty products that get thrown away in the decluttering process is often staggering. While the $300,000 that an average American woman will spend on facial products in a lifetime seems impossible, the website pictures make it a bit more plausible.

One way we can combat this bombardment of advertising messages is to become aware of and practice tactics that nurture us, thereby reassuring us that we are enough. I do this by listening to the majesty of a bird symphony, watching sunrises and sunsets, walking along the beach, wandering among trees, basking in the aroma of nature, floating in the ocean surf, connecting with friends, strolling through an art exhibit, and traveling our vast nation and distant lands. It's helpful to be aware of things that bring you joy, so you can draw on them when you feel depleted.

In those rare times when I don't feel like I'm enough or don't have enough, my feelings impact all aspects of my life. Not only is my worldview skewed toward scarcity, but I can't do everyday tasks, like cleaning out closets. As I've observed my behavior through the years, I find that when I don't have enough money to replace the clothes I'd otherwise donate, my scarcity mentality creates fear that keeps me from removing them from my closet. I'm frozen as I think, *At least this dress would give me something to wear for a specific occasion for which I don't have the money to buy something new*, or *It doesn't fit now, but I really like it, and maybe I'll lose enough weight to get back into it.*

Each decision becomes a conversation inside my head that eventually causes me to give up on cleaning out my closet altogether.

On the other hand, when attempting the same task from a place of abundance, I find that removing the element of fear around replacing items allows me to easily make decisions about what I want to keep and what can go. This example reveals how feelings around having enough and being enough can create a vicious cycle: The sense of scarcity breeds doubt, doubt leads to fear (that we aren't enough or don't have enough), and fear influences decisions that reinforce scarcity. If I can't trust that I have enough or that I *am* enough, I experience fear that I will ever be or have enough.

Let's look at some stories that reveal the pain that results from feelings of fear and insecurity.

My Story

I was struck by evidence of my metamorphosis from a scarcity to an abundance mentality as a result of Covid-19. I started biting my nails when I was a young child, patterning my mom's habit. My grandmother did all she could to help me stop, including offering me a reward of $100 when I was in high school (a lot of money at the time). I tried many ways to remind myself that I no longer wanted to bite them, from placing a rubber band on my wrist that I snapped each time I found my fingers in my mouth to putting a disgusting liquid on my nails. I ate right through it, and I never got the $100.

Fast forward many decades, and the fashionable gel nails I'd worn for many years could no longer be applied because

Covid-19 had forced nail salons to close. Only when I chipped my front tooth biting my nails (old habits die hard) did I tell myself this had to stop! After a few months, my nails were longer and stronger than they'd ever been in my life. They were so long that they needed to be clipped rather than filed. Did I dare cut these nails that felt like they had taken a lifetime to grow? They were so strong that it was difficult for the nail clippers to make the cut. And then, in that instant, I knew. Not only had my nails grown, I'd grown too. My heart overflowed with a sense of abundance as I knew I could cut them and trust that I would let them grow again. And I did.

››› *Maggie*

> Sometimes a single event around money causes a trauma so deep that kids spend a lifetime striving to avoid memories of their childhood experiences. Maggie, whose parents struggled throughout her childhood with credit card debt, can't bear the thought of having access to a credit card, even though she's highly responsible about managing her finances. She explains that having a credit card gives her a sensation of fear just from seeing the card in her wallet. As we've worked together for several years, she's been able to acknowledge the basis of her fear, along with her ability to use a credit card sensibly and wisely—and the recognition that having at least one credit card is necessary in the world we live in. Still, she has to force herself to use it so she can build her credit score.

››› *The Milton Family*

Members of the same family often have different memories of an experience they all witnessed. The Milton family hit a rough patch when their kids were in elementary school. Clara and Gary had a thriving home-building business that Clara inherited from her parents. Home building is cyclical in nature, and those whose businesses survive the unexpected downturns know the value of having cash reserves to weather future storms.

In late 2008, the Miltons' business ground to a halt when buyers couldn't get home mortgages. They had a sizable inventory of new homes they hadn't yet completed and finished ones that hadn't sold. As the mortgage crisis dragged on, they faced other large family expenses, and they soon found that their savings were insufficient to maintain their lifestyle. Tension built between Clara and Gary as Clara took on the added fear and guilt of potentially losing the business she'd inherited after watching her parents struggle to build it. Gary had made a decision to fund the growth of the business with debt before the financial crash. Clara had questioned his decision at the time but went along with his enthusiasm for their bright future. "If we aren't going forward, we're going backward," Gary would say. Now she felt resentment toward him and anger at herself for going along with ideas she didn't fully support.

As their parents argued over finances, nine-year-old Jamie and eleven-year-old Ben listened. Even when they weren't arguing, the kids could feel the tension in the air. The stress permeated their home, but each of the kids experienced it differently. Jamie absorbed the tension as her fear mounted. She would go to her room and close the door to block the sound of her parents' yelling, reading books to her dolls and talking to them about her fear that her parents might divorce. As she reached adulthood and earned a good salary, she remembered her fear as a kid and doubted if her savings would be enough to cover her basic needs if disaster struck. She had a sense that no amount would be enough to feel safe. As a single woman with few expenses, she built a sizable savings account. As the stock market soared, she knew she was missing out on the opportunity to make significant returns on her money, but her fear of the potential loss of what she had worked so hard to gain kept her from investing. When she made major purchases, like her first new car, her hands would sweat and her heart would beat faster as she thought about how paying the car's purchase price would reduce the balance in her savings account. She described her relationship with money as "tortured."

Shortly after buying her new car, Jamie and Ben spent a weekend hanging out at their grandparents' lake cottage. Over a glass of wine, they discussed Jamie's emotional reaction to buying the car. As she related what she described to her brother as a "dreadful experience," Ben asked why she thought she had such a visceral reaction to something as simple as buying a car that she could well afford. She couldn't imagine why he would ask a question with such an obvious answer when he'd grown up listening to the same arguments between their parents as she had. He said, "Sure, they argued, but don't all parents argue? I never thought it was any big deal." Contrary to Jamie's experience, Ben didn't absorb their parents' arguments the way Jamie did that created her sense of scarcity. Nor did he understand why he had a healthier relationship with money than she did.

A plethora of factors influence how we experience events that took place during our childhood, and the memories and consequences of those events. Age, gender, sensitivity, and birth order are but a few. In general, Jamie's personality tends toward empathy, absorbing the pain of others, while Ben lets things roll off his back. Ben developed an abundance mentality, while Jamie felt scarcity deep in her soul. The reality of their childhood was identical, but their experiences and memories were quite different. The consequences of those experiences created divergent paths for both of them.

The Milton kids help us understand a difference I've observed in clients and friends as they consider how much money they need to feel secure. Confidence in our ability to respond to whatever might happen seems to be a driving force behind our belief that we have enough. Sometimes, it's difficult to feel financially secure, regardless of the amount of money we have. I've watched clients raise the bar on the amount of money they'll need to feel secure as their careers advance and they earn more. As they make more money, they tend to amass more, bigger, and pricier things. Therefore, they feel the need to have more money in reserve to avoid the potential of losing what they've worked so hard to gain. It's a vicious cycle. Interestingly, it appears that Gen Y and Z could change the trajectory of this pattern, as they tend to prefer buying experiences over things and lean toward minimalism.

››› *Kathrine*

Maybe we have in mind a dollar amount that would free us from being financially stressed. We've answered for ourselves the question: "How much is enough to feel financially secure?" I watched this unfold over several years as my friend Kathrine told me, when we were both in our mid-thirties, "If I had $100,000 in the bank, then I'd feel financially set for life." As a single professional homeowner with a six-figure salary and no children, she amassed $100,000 in her retirement account within a few years. Still, she said that didn't make her feel secure because it was saved for retirement. So she continued contributing to her 401(k), eventually growing it to $275,000, and she built her savings account to an additional $150,000.

Apparently forgetting her earlier comment and ignoring her retirement investments that had performed well, one day she remarked, "If I had $200,000 in the bank, I'd feel financially secure. I'm almost there." She thought her sense of security was tied to a movable target that she kept changing. I reminded her that she'd once said the same thing about having $100,000 in reserve, and now, with more than double that amount in her retirement fund alone, she was telling me she didn't have enough to feel secure. Again, she declared the retirement money "couldn't be included." We had a good laugh as we discussed that she could choose not to include the retirement money in her thinking about the value of her net worth, but she *had* the money in her accounts. She could also choose to feel secure or not, but it was likely that she would continue to raise the bar as she gained more responsible positions with accompanying higher salaries and she accumulated more wealth.

The concept of "enough" is a relative one that carries significant emotional weight. When our confidence is tied to a specific amount of money, we find ourselves continually moving the target, just as Kathrine did. But when our confidence comes from our inner ability to weather whatever storms might befall us or to cope with adversity, then the dollar amount has less significance in creating a feeling of security.

As a society whose members obsessed over buying toilet paper during the Covid pandemic, the underlying fear of not having enough was profoundly revealed. Talk about scarcity mentality! The message created something akin to a mob mentality of scarcity: *If others buy too much toilet paper, there might not be enough for me when I need it, so I need to protect myself and my family from the unimaginable disaster of doing without and not being able to get more.*

As you reflect on what it means to have (and be) enough and the role it plays in your beliefs around money, I encourage you to consider how you're influenced by advertising messages that have nothing to do with your reality. You might want to notice aspects of these different stories that you see in yourself. Consider how your awareness can lead to understanding how you might do things differently to achieve an outcome that moves you toward having the healthier, more constructive, peaceful relationship with your money that you desire.

SOMETHING TO THINK ABOUT

- What are some things that nourish your soul when you feel depleted?
- In what ways do you succumb to the beauty industry's messages of unattainable beauty standards?
- Can you identify specific feelings (perhaps anger, fear, or dread) that result from memories related to financial issues in your childhood?
- As you think about having enough, what do you use to measure what you have, need, and want?
- As you think about "enough," what factors do you consider? Money? Time? Experiences? Possessions? Accomplishments? Health? Overall well-being? Other factors?
- What specific amount in savings would you like to have to feel financially secure by the time you retire?
- If you have a life partner, how do you think they might answer these same questions? How do the differences in your answers get played out in your relationship?

Chapter 12

Why Not a Budget?

Before we go any further, you might be curious about why I don't recommend budgets to clients.

It may seem like heresy for a financial professional not to recommend having a budget, but please hear me out. While budgets can be meaningful, they are most useful for people who don't need the rigor of constraints to manage their finances. I understand that some folks actually enjoy creating budgets to set goals and provide internal accountability as they accomplish them, but for the rest of us, the term "budget" is to spending what "diet" is to eating.

In the same way that people who eat reasonably, are physically fit, and are in good health don't need diets, people who handle their finances responsibly and with little stress don't need budgets—at least not as a tool to manage their money, especially when they don't want to create or maintain one. In first meetings, more than one client has told me they know they need a budget, as if they assume that I expect them to have one and might see them as being financially irresponsible by virtue of not having one. I often hear a deep sigh of relief when I tell them I doubt they need a budget, and that they likely don't need to create one more to-do item that adds stress to their lives.

I differentiate between a budget, which tends to be restrictive, and a spending plan, which is empowering. While I fully support using a spending plan to guide purchasing and financial decisions, I caution against the use of a traditional budget. It might seem like a difference in semantics, but a budget can feel constraining, often leading to financial stress while making it harder to manage finances with ease and confidence. Instead, a spending plan offers flexibility and allows for thoughtful, informed decisions without the pressure of constant limitation.

This comparison between food and money becomes important when we consider the negative impact of dieting, something that is rarely successful over the long haul when it's used to attempt to permanently alter our behavior. Budgets have a similar result. Both harken to deprivation, shame, guilt, evidence of lack of self-control, and self-loathing, and they send us a message that we're incapable of doing what is best for our own well-being. As with overeating and focusing on restrictive nutritional details of food, budgets often start with a belief that we need them to rein in spending.

Why would we create one more personal monster that chips away at our self-esteem? If we want to have a healthy relationship with our money, we don't need our negative self-talk yipping inside our heads. I like to think of my monster as a creature who sits on my shoulder, just next to my ear. When I realize he's chattering away (yes, mine is a *he*), I thank him for being concerned about my well-being and remind him that his concerns might have been valid at an earlier time in my life when they protected me, but I no longer want or need his protection. I tell him he's not welcome and ask him to go sit in a chair, far away from my ear. I find this more helpful than thinking I can banish him once and for all. He's been with me too long to easily be abandoned.

Merriam-Webster defines a budget as "a plan for the coordination of resources and expenditures." This sounds innocuous, but as with most things related to money, it can take on a life of its own, with accompanying emotional fall-out. Often the assumption that we need a budget comes from parents, both those who have budgets and those who don't. For parents who have organized their financial lives around a budget, they often assume that their children need to do the same to prove that they are responsible with money. Parents who don't have a budget often think they would have more control over their finances *if only* they had one, and therefore assume their adult children need a budget to be able to control their money—in the "do as I say, not as I do" model of parenting.

Because of the baggage around the word "budget," let's agree to dismiss the idea. You can tell your parents you read this in a book—that should give you some degree of cover if you need it. Let's instead talk about a spending plan. This term better describes the benefits of having a method to "coordinate your resources and expenditures," as the definition describes, and removes the negative emotions around the term "budget."

To better understand the difference between a budget and a spending plan, let's watch how it played out for Allye and Robert Tuma, two of many clients who talked of needing a budget at our first meeting.

››› *Robert and Allye Tuma*

While Robert and Allye's financial situation allowed them to spend more money than many of us would have available, the process we developed to manage their spending applied the same, regardless of the amount they had to spend. When we first started working together over a decade ago, Robert insisted on creating a budget to gain control of family spending. I worked with him and Allye to analyze their spending by category during the previous year. As we reviewed the results of my report, Robert focused on the total amount they had spent, saying, "This is too much." He didn't want to spend more than a specified amount that he considered to be a reasonable number, an amount that was significantly less than what their family had spent the previous year.

I was asked to provide insight into which categories they might focus on to reduce their spending. The largest discretionary categories would require them to significantly cut back on family vacations, recreational activities, clothes, and accessories. When I presented my findings, they thought the reductions within each category were reasonable and said they would work toward spending the "budgeted" amount.

From my perspective, this budgeting process was of no benefit to them. In the first place, this family had the income and resources to be able to spend what they were spending. Robert had an emotional reaction when he first saw the total amount they had spent the previous year. Their spending wasn't driving them to financial insecurity, causing conflict in their marriage, keeping them from investing excess funds in the market, or negatively impacting their philanthropic efforts. As I've described, Robert thought the amount they spent was simply "too much." As we've now worked together for many years, he's gotten comfortable with knowing the monthly amounts they are spending but not using them to curtail their quality of life. Rather than a budget, they have a spending plan that provides useful information when making financial choices.

To create a spending plan, it is helpful to know how much you're spending within specific categories, just as I calculated for the Tumas. This first step is crucial to gain a clear picture of your financial habits. With this awareness, you can make informed decisions about whether, and how, to adjust your spending to align with your goals. Just as with Allye and Robert, for some, it's possible that simply knowing where their money is going can be enough to provide a sense of security and control.

››› *Jan*

One of my early clients, Jan, with whom I've now worked for more than twenty years, also started our first meeting by insisting that she needed a budget. She had struggled with everything related to money, from paying her bills on time to managing spending and overusing credit cards, and was convinced that if she had a budget, all her financial woes would disappear. As I listened to her describe the ways she thought about money, I suspected a budget would only add to her stress and self-described sense of financial ineptitude.

She told me how her dad was an accountant who could never keep a job. She'd attended thirteen schools in twelve years as they'd moved to yet another new town because her dad had been fired and they were ostracized in the small towns where they lived. As an adult, she concluded that he had Attention Deficit Disorder, which she believed she had inherited and thought was driving her difficulties around money. She thought a budget could provide structure that would constrain her spending and provide a method to see her finances in a way she could better understand how to manage them.

Jan had tried numerous methods to control her finances. For example, she carried several envelopes in her purse that contained cash to be used for specific purposes—one for groceries, one for paper products, one for cleaning supplies, one for clothes. You can imagine how cumbersome this system was and why it didn't work, especially for someone who had trouble keeping things sequential in her mind. I don't think it's an overstatement to say she was desperate to find a process that would give her a sense of peace. I knew a budget was not the answer.

I could see that Jan's difficulty in handling her finances could eventually result in losing her ability to live independently, as she might exhaust her finite financial resources if she lived a long life. One area that caused her most immediate concern was that she regularly got cut-off notices from utility companies for nonpayment. The first thing we accomplished together was to set up her utilities with autopayments. The second step was to replace her credit cards with debit cards so that she paid at the time she bought items rather than having to remember to pay the statement when it arrived.

She feared opening mail so much that she ignored it, which created unpaid utilities, ignored credit card statements, and delinquent payments to the IRS, resulting in hundreds of dollars of unnecessary penalties, late fees, and interest over time. For Jan, a budget would have served no purpose other than to exacerbate her belief that she wasn't capable of handling her money in the way she wanted to.

As we reviewed her monthly financial reports, she saw the benefits of knowing she had spent within her self-determined plan and avoided the debilitating self-talk she previously experienced after having her utilities turned off. As she changed her processes around money and the way she saw herself having financial control, her spending plan accomplished far more than a budget ever could have.

If you're not convinced of the negative aspects of a budget yet, let's talk about how you might think a budget could be beneficial. If you find that having a budget helps you manage your money, I'm not suggesting you stop doing what's working for you. If it's a process you enjoy using, by all means, carry on! You might even want to skip the rest of this chapter.

Rather, I'm talking to those of you who have been told by others, or believe yourselves, that a budget might improve your relationship with your money. Let's investigate your thoughts about needing a budget. How might you answer these questions?

- Does having a budget create a sense of being a financially responsible adult?
- Is it something your parents did, and therefore you think you should do as well, perhaps to gain their approval?
- If you're a young adult, do your parents expect you to have a budget as proof that you're ready to live on your own?
- Do you think you need a budget to know where your money goes?
- Do you ask, *Where did it all go?* when you see your year-end tax statements? Is that when you think about needing a budget to understand where you spend your money?
- Do you think a budget will provide guardrails to help you reduce your spending?

If you hope a budget will provide answers to these questions, I invite you to think about other ways to accomplish similar goals. You know yourself and what works for you better than anyone else. Perhaps using different time horizons as you think about spending would "click" for you. For example, Joan treats herself to a $5 drink at Starbucks every day with money she can certainly afford to spend. However, she hasn't considered that if she gets a $5 drink every day, over the course of the year, she'll spend over $1,800. She might also consider that same amount over five years ($9,000) or ten years ($18,000). Thinking about what she could do with $18,000 provides a different perspective than thinking of her drink as "only" costing $5 a day, doesn't it?

If you typically think of your spending habits in smaller chunks—like how much you're spending per day—this example shows that it can also be helpful to look at the bigger picture. Some folks prefer to analyze spending information on a monthly or annual basis, while others prefer to think about it weekly or even daily. Whatever method is beneficial to you, calculating those amounts using different time horizons can provide insights into overall spending, as well.

Fortunately, technology can provide an assortment of tools to help you track spending without investing a lot of time in the process. While some people prefer to use spreadsheets, I don't recommend them because of the time they take to maintain. I like to use Quicken, as it gives me the ability to easily customize categories for tracking purchases in whatever way is meaningful to each client. While some people use Quicken primarily as a check register and bill payment tool, I find its most useful aspect to be the reporting functions. Reports are automatically generated from the data that's been entered into the check register and allow you to compare spending by category (groceries, clothing, car expenses, kid expenses, rent/mortgage, etc.) over a variety of different time periods. If you choose to have Quicken download transactions from your different accounts, it will assign purchases to assumed categories.

Other options, such as Mint, Goodbudget, EveryDollar, You Need A Budget (YNAB), PocketGuard, Copilot, and others, are designed to automatically assign expenses to categories to help track where your money goes. In our primarily cashless society, people tend to use credit, debit, or ATM cards or money-transfer platforms like Apple Pay, Google Pay, Venmo, PayPal, and Zelle for most daily purchases or money transfers between people. Many of these tools allow technology to give a detailed map of where our money goes and require little or no effort on our part to have the information in a useful format that can influence and inform our spending.

If you're still open to considering my argument for not having a budget and replacing it with a spending plan, I encourage you to reflect on four important things you need to know, regardless of the process that works best for you:

- where you spend your money, identified by specific categories
- how much you spend overall and by category
- how your spending compares to your income
- categories where you can cut back if you want to reduce your spending

Furthermore, I encourage you to consider the other benefits of having a spending plan and maintaining financial records so that they're easily accessible when you need them to provide:

- informed knowledge about your finances and spending habits
- a tool to help you reduce debt and/or spending
- awareness of what you have available for savings and retirement
- accurate information to assist in identifying and informing financial goals
- a scorecard to know how you're doing financially from your own perspective
- a reasonable amount to have on hand for emergencies
- information to assess how much you have available for a reserve fund (financial guru Suze Orman recommends enough to cover eight months of living expenses)
- information easily accessible for calculating income taxes

SOMETHING TO THINK ABOUT

- What is your reaction to the word "budget"?
- Did you grow up in a home where your parents used a budget? If so, did they discuss it with you? Did/do they recommend that you have one?
- Before reading this chapter, did you think, *If I had a budget, I'd be able to control my spending better*?
- Do you think a spending plan could help manage your finances, whereas a budget seems unappealing?
- As you read this chapter, what emotions rose to the surface?

Chapter 13

When Our Financial World Turns Upside Down

Finances have always been cyclical, as humankind has experienced for centuries. From the first recorded financial crisis of AD 33, through the fourteenth-century banking crisis, to the downfall of Tulip Mania in the seventeenth century, to the Irish Potato Famine—aka the Great Hunger—that began in 1845 and lasted six years, and through multiple crises of subsequent centuries, civilization has suffered financial downturns and ultimately survived. But individuals and families often paid a terrible price for that survival, and of course, some didn't survive.

For decades, we've been hearing that a large segment of American workers live paycheck to paycheck. Throughout the Covid-19 pandemic, stories filled the news of people who had no financial cushion, or who perhaps had just enough money to pay bills for one or two months before they faced financial devastation. The miles and miles of cars lined up to get free food spoke volumes about the financial trauma experienced by many.

The international tariffs threatened, imposed, removed, and reinstated by Donald Trump in 2025 caused whiplash for Americans who watched retirement and investment accounts ride a roller coaster of values. As I write this, the fallout from the Department of Government Efficiency's massive governmental layoffs and economic policies is causing panic and financial chaos for many Americans. As I think about workers who believed they had secure jobs and suddenly had hours to clear out their personal belongings as they were locked out of their computers and desks, my heart aches for the turmoil I imagine they and their families are facing.

Many factors determine how people react to financial loss, and the reactions vary greatly, often depending on memories from one's own childhood. If a child who experienced hearing that their father had been laid off saw firsthand how that news impacted their family, they're likely to have similar feelings when their husband or wife walks through the door with similar news.

As with other types of loss, emotions come in phases, not unlike those of grief around death. For many, the loss of a job likely feels somewhat like a sudden death. One day we think our lives are going well, and the next, entire departments or agencies are laid off, projects are canceled, businesses are closed, industry sectors are no longer marketable, and jobs evaporate overnight. The cascading effect of a lost job can result in significant lifestyle changes, often starting with the loss of health insurance at a time when many need it most. Renters can't pay rent, and homeowners can't pay mortgages. From there, the results can feel like free-falling when physical survival becomes the primary concern overnight.

Because I have experienced both the sudden death of my beloved grandmother, who passed away during a conversation over a cup of coffee, and the slow death of my mom due to dementia, I know some of the ways our bodies and minds react to the experiences of loss. For some whose financial lives have been upended by death, pandemic, natural disasters, fires, sudden disability, divorce, recession, bankruptcy, or any other unexpected event, they have experienced the suddenness of loss, similar to the death of my grandmother. For others, whose circumstances created a longer, drawn-out downturn, it has likely been more like a slow decline and ultimate death similar to losing my mom, as I watched her quality of life and the person I knew fade away as her dementia worsened.

My friends, family, and clients provide a window into a tiny segment of American experiences around money during major financial downturns—some who lost hundreds of thousands of dollars in the financial market crashes caused by the dot-com bubble (2000), 9/11 terrorist attack (2001), housing market collapse (2008), and pandemic (2020). Some clients sold their stock portfolios as they watched the value decline precipitously and, therefore, lost the opportunity to recoup their losses when the market rebounded. A client who received a large lump-sum divorce settlement discovered that the market downturn and excessive spending subsequently rendered her homeless.

I observe my clients' patterns from the perspective of being a process-oriented sociologist by training. I am therefore curious about patterns of behavior as I try to understand what's happening at both psychological and societal levels. Let's look at some snapshots of the ways various people responded to the financial upheaval caused by Covid-19.

Covid-19 Responses

Carrie and Janie, both single women in their sixties and seventies, respectively, are retired with lifetime pensions, and both had little anxiety related to the pandemic. Since they didn't need their investments to augment daily living expenses, they were confident that the Covid-19 economy would rebound before it significantly impacted them. Most didn't fare so well.

Jason, twenty-two, worked at a small business where everyone took a significantly reduced salary to help save the jobs of all the employees during the early days of the pandemic, as the company expected a downturn in sales. He stressed over how his reduced salary meant forgoing payments into his 401(k) plan. Mitchell worked in a retail store and was laid off because his work wasn't deemed essential, a term that became critical to job security during the pandemic. Even though he immediately filed for unemployment benefits, they didn't cover his rent in the San Francisco Bay Area, let alone provide food and other necessities. Lindsay, soon to graduate college, feared starting her career at a time when companies were closing or had hiring freezes. Matt, a small business owner with fifty employees, had concerns about being able to make payroll and felt responsible for the families of his employees.

Still others quit their jobs, receiving more money from government assistance programs than they could earn while working. The result of losing employees caused many restaurants, service companies, and retail stores to struggle—or close—when they would have otherwise remained open if they had staff available.

Francine and Judy

As owner of a fledgling fitness training business, Francine offered classes from a friend's studio. When she could no longer teach on-site classes because of the Covid shutdown, she changed her business model to online teaching. At nearly sixty, she struggled with a significant technological learning curve but soon found that she had new students from all over the country, more than the number who ever could have fit in the studio at one time.

As her student base grew, Francine was excited about the opportunities the new business model presented. Seeing her revenue increase, she thought she was on the cusp of a thriving business beyond any she'd ever imagined. She asked her current students to promote her classes to their friends to add more newcomers. When they didn't materialize, she sought to increase her revenue by nearly doubling prices for some—but not all—students, quoting different rates to different students for the same classes and telling students they were paying the same prices as others, even though they weren't.

As her student Judy shared her observations to another class member, she mentioned that she could feel the negative energy of Francine's anxiety around her financial situation. She added that she felt tension in Francine's emails regarding payments and pricing. Therefore, she decided to stop training with Francine. As Judy discussed her departure with other students who had become personal friends, they told her they would also stop their

> training if Francine increased their prices. Francine created a situation that was both unfortunate and unnecessary. Her reaction gives us insight into how the pandemic impacted her finances, while revealing a deep-seated scarcity mentality that eventually led to the demise of her business.

People processed their beliefs, fears, and emotions around money differently during the pandemic. Often, their stories of fear and deprivation reminded me of others whose parents or grandparents grew up during the Great Depression. The Covid-19 pandemic created a generation of children whose ways of thinking about money will forever be impacted by their experiences during these difficult times, just as the Great Depression did. Additionally, well-documented and widely observed consequences of attending online classes have affected academic, social, emotional, and developmental domains.

Through the years, I've watched as emotions around money drive clients to one extreme or another. For some who have a finite amount of money (typically from inheritance, divorce settlements, or retirement funds), the fear of exhausting their financial reserves causes a need for austerity, so they spend only what's required for the most basic essentials of living. As we saw in Chapter Six, Jim had saved for retirement throughout his life, but when he needed to dip into those funds, he agonized over each phone call to his broker to access his own money.

On the other hand, some report spending money furiously in anticipation of their potential financial demise. Two clients who will never physically be able to work again and who have limited familial support systems, and have a finite amount of money to last the rest of their lives, have told me they'll end their lives when their money is gone. In contrast, others whose financial resources are limited, but not finite, are confident that their lifetime needs will be met. For some, religious beliefs provide assurance that they and their families will survive whatever comes, while for others, faith in oneself provides confidence that they will endure. Still others have a financial plan that reassures them they will be able to withstand difficult times. The way we think about money plays a significant role in both our confidence to weather an impending storm and in our coping strategies. Among other issues, changes in the economy remind us of the importance of knowing ourselves in relation to our finances and having open lines of communication with significant others in our lives.

SOMETHING TO THINK ABOUT

- What is your pattern of response to uncertainty?
- What, if anything, do you need from others during uncertain times?
- How have life events shaped your thinking about your future in the event of unexpected hardship?
- How do you think these experiences might influence your future financial decisions?
- If you have a life partner, in what ways are your coping strategies similar? Different?
- What types of life events create a sense of fear for you?

PART III:

Money Within Families

Working with three generations within several families gives me a window into the intergenerational consequences of ideas about money that are passed down from one generation to the next.

Familial patterns of thinking about money have a significant influence on subsequent generations and are often carried forward, especially when money isn't discussed overtly. If we want to break the patterns we've learned from previous generations, we need to be intentional about identifying the changes in our behavior that we must make. Kids seem to either follow in their parents' footsteps or bounce off them like a basketball. As for my personal journey, I took the basketball approach and decided as a teenager that I would not live my life consumed with worry about money, as my mom had. Even though I tried not to follow her patterns, I did—until I didn't. Let's look at some ways these influences impact our families, both those we were born into and those we create.

Chapter 14

Partners and Money

If you have a visceral reaction when you think about money in relation to your life partner, you might want to take several deep breaths now. It's helpful to consider where you are in the relationship as you think about how you and your partner deal with money, either together or separately. If you're in a new relationship, maybe one you wouldn't yet define as a partnership, you might want to think about previous relationships and how money issues impacted them. Or perhaps you've been together for decades and always handled money one way, with little or no consideration about the way you do things. Of course, if what you're doing is working, there's no need to fix what's not broken.

Strategies around handling money might need to change as relationships evolve. If you find that you want to change the way you and your partner handle finances, prepare yourself for some resistance. In the following stories, you'll see why it's important to understand what you think about money and how you want your finances to relate to those of your partner. As you contemplate the "how" of your joint finances, you might want to consider whether dependency plays a role, and if so, how that dependency may have changed over the time you've been together. As we'll see in this chapter, there is no "right" or "wrong" way of thinking about shared finances. I would never suggest a specific strategy, such as combining finances or keeping them separate. We'll see in the following stories how both approaches can work well when you communicate. Open and consistent communication is more important than your choice about a system to handle finances.

After examining your own ideas, you will want to engage your partner in a discussion to see where your ideas are similar or contradictory. Discuss the underlying reasons for your differences and reflect on how they affect your relationship now. Identify changes you'd like to see in the future. Especially if you've been together a long time, you might think you know what your partner will say, but I encourage you to ask questions to see if your assumptions are correct. Questions at the end of the chapter will guide your thinking, as well as provide prompts for discussions with your partner.

If finances cause stress in your relationship, it will be important to try to keep judgment out of your tone of voice. After some discussion, perhaps you'll decide that you would like a different outcome around money in your relationship, and begin thinking about how you might accomplish that goal. I encourage you to remember that this is a journey, and what works for you in your current situation most likely needs to be fluid so it can evolve as your relationship changes. By discussing your finances, you create a foundation from which you can make adjustments to your process as things change over time. Be gentle with yourself and your partner as you choose the timing and setting for these conversations, so they'll be more likely to have the best outcome.

When consulting couples, I find those who were raised in financially secure homes (financial "haves," I call them) often unite in partnership with those who were not raised in such homes (financial "have nots"). For our purposes, the terms "have" and "have not" refer to having access to the opportunities that money can afford us vs. not having those same opportunities due to a lack of funds. I'm not suggesting that money is the only unit of analysis that creates a sense of having or not having what we need. For example, although I was a financial "have not" for a significant part of my life, I enjoyed many opportunities that would classify me as a "have" in other areas. I was loved, nurtured, and encouraged to fulfill my dreams. I enjoyed good health, benefited from a good quality education, and had the wonderful good fortune of going on road trips with my grandparents. I was encouraged to develop personal attributes like good character, perseverance, healthy ambition, and the ability to make things happen. In all these ways and more, I consider myself a "have," but I grew up in a home where a lack of money permeated every decision my mom made. Thus, I knew from a young age that I was at the mercy of her decisions. Financially, I was a "have not."

The dichotomy between partners being financial "haves" and "have nots" certainly fits my own marriage. My husband, Kent, grew up in what I would have considered an affluent home. In reality, it was only slightly upper-middle-class, not what I would call "affluent" today. On the other hand, our household had none of the finer things, and we couldn't afford activities beyond basic living. Kent's parents took their family of seven to restaurants and the theater, to major sporting events, and on family vacations, sometimes international ones. The kids attended a variety of summer camps and participated in extracurricular activities that cost money, things my family couldn't provide. They got new clothes when they wanted them, rather than only when they'd outgrown old ones.

The only times I dined at restaurants were when my grandparents would "treat" us, and I never took a vacation anywhere with my mom. If an extracurricular activity included the need for a fee or a uniform, I only participated if my grandparents paid for these requirements. Therefore, it's no surprise that money was the topic of the first argument Kent and I had, when he questioned why I'd bought myself a pink pantsuit, even though I'd paid for it with money I'd earned myself. As I think about it now, I remember that my stepdad displayed his disapproval when I used my work earnings while in high school to buy myself school clothes. I have no doubt that my teenage experience caused Kent's question to become a trigger to which I didn't respond well. I could have rebutted with humor to defuse the situation, but instead, I reacted in anger.

When I married Kent, I was a fiercely independent, accomplished woman in my mid-twenties. I had a good job as an office manager and owned my home, which I'd remodeled and furnished, and a nice car. Therefore, when Kent questioned my buying the pantsuit a couple of weeks after our wedding, I told him that I didn't have to explain my purchasing decisions to him. I'll explain later how we came to be married just a month after our first date, but because our courtship was so quick, we hadn't had time to cover the basics of how we might share our life together, and money certainly wasn't part of our limited conversations.

I mistakenly assumed Kent had a significant amount

of money because he seemed to have endless financial resources. It appeared to me that money afforded him the ability to do whatever he wanted. In the days when we kept a paper check register, I noticed that he never wrote the remaining balance in his checkbook after writing a check. Given that I wrote the balance after every check to know how much money was in my account at all times, the only reason I could imagine for not doing so was that he had so much money, he didn't need to worry about his ongoing balance. What I didn't know was that if he overdrafted his bank account, the family banker at the Dallas Mercantile Bank would call his dad, and his dad would tell the banker to move money from his account into Kent's to cover the shortfall. Then Kent would reimburse him when he got his next paycheck. (I would add that younger readers might well have no idea what I'm talking about, as they may not have written checks, and certainly don't need to keep a check register to track their bank balances.)

Today, we chuckle at my erroneous assumptions. While it's funny to us, for many couples, a similar beginning could have ended in divorce. Kent and I have not had another argument over my purchasing decisions since that first one more than fifty years ago, nor have I questioned his decisions. While arguing over specific purchases is often a source of conflict between partners, I think our lack of arguments about money speaks to our mutual trust that neither of us would spend money on something that would put our family in financial jeopardy.

Nevertheless, rare is the couple that doesn't argue over money. Often, an argument appears to be about the financial decision of the moment, when it is really over deeper misunderstandings, like a scarcity vs. abundance mentality, starting in childhood.

Are you familiar with those paint-by-number kits that tell you step-by-step what color to put on the cardboard canvas next? Similarly, sometimes Kent and I "argue by number" when we've had the same disagreement repeatedly. We can merely say "forty-nine" and know this is the argument about a specific topic we've had many times before. Sometimes we argue because it seems easier to focus on money than to deal with more painful issues that lie beneath the surface discussion. We know this argument is safe because we've had it so often that previous experience tells us nothing dreadful will happen from having it yet again.

Let's look at some different ways of handling joint finances that have either worked well or not. As we'll see, the specific situation of each couple significantly impacts whether the system they use around combining or separating finances works well or leads to problems. My intention is for these stories to provide you with food for thought about your own situation. I intend no judgment toward the people involved or the reasons they handle their finances the way they do.

››› *Noah and Ava*

Noah attended one of my community talks about money, "How to Have 'The Talk,'" which focused on the importance of discussing financial matters with partners. He described shopping for a sofa with his partner, Ava. They had recently bought their first home together and were looking forward to furnishing it. As they stood in the furniture store considering which sofa to buy, their conversation dissolved into an argument, which resulted in their leaving the store without buying anything. After they calmed down, they discussed what had happened. Ava believed they should buy an inexpensive sofa since they needed to buy a houseful of furniture. She thought it would be wise to spend the least amount possible on each item so their money would go further. Noah, on the other hand, grew up in a home where his parents still used most of the furniture they'd bought or been given early in their marriage. Therefore, the model he grew up with suggested that he and Ava should buy the most expensive sofa they could afford, assuming it would last longer and be a better long-term use of their money. As they stood in the store, these weren't the issues they raised; instead, they appeared to be arguing over different styles and colors of sofas, rather than the underlying issues that were driving their emotions.

This example illustrates the cost of not talking about the subtle messages we carry about money and purchasing decisions. If we don't know whether our beliefs are our own or carryovers from our parents, we'll continue having arguments about whether to buy a blue plaid or green striped sofa, rather than discovering how and why we make the financial decisions we do.

Before a meaningful relationship moves from dating to something more permanent, we should engage in discussions about money. When two people come together, often with little introspection about what they believe and how those beliefs impact their decision-making process, it's no surprise that arguments often erupt, even on an outing to select a sofa.

We'll see from the stories that follow that both keeping finances separate and commingling them can work well for couples. Conversations about money during the dating process will impact how we handle finances as the relationship evolves. Knowing our underlying beliefs is important to both our own relationship with money and those we have with others.

After we've discussed the broader ideas and experiences around money with our partner, it's easier to delve into the more detailed logistics of handling joint finances. I've been privileged to observe the various ways in which couples have found what works best for them—ways that reaffirm that there's no single right or wrong way to merge money, or not to merge it. Let's look at some of the different ways my clients live together financially.

››› *Tala and Jacob, Timur and Gloria*

> We met Tala in Chapter Eight when we talked about gender inequality. She is one of those rare women whose dad, Timur, taught her about money from a young age. As immigrants from a poor country in the Far East, Timur and his wife, Gloria, arrived in the United States not knowing what a credit card was. They started their new life in a new country, making ends meet by starting at the bottom of the career ladder. Eventually, Timur became a real estate entrepreneur in a booming Bay Area market, and Gloria had a rewarding middle-management career. Timur was intentional about teaching his young daughter the many things he had to learn quickly about money after he'd arrived—things he

needed to know not only to survive but to thrive in the United States.

As a young married adult, their daughter Tala was self-sufficient, with a good job in the investment brokerage industry. After being divorced for some years, she met Jacob, who was a few years older, further advanced in his career, and therefore had more money than she did. Because of her experience with her first husband, she didn't want the disparity in their income to become a source of problems between them, even though the gender roles were reversed from those of her first marriage in that Jacob was the higher income earner. She told me she felt like she needed to prove to Jacob that she wasn't with him for his money. Therefore, after a couple of dates where he paid, she insisted on either splitting their dinner checks or alternating who paid for their meals. Although she enjoyed being part of his more lavish lifestyle, she quickly learned that his taste for fine wines and expensive dining was more than she could afford. After paying for several meals, she broached the issue with him. He asked, "What *can* you afford?" to which she replied, "Burritos." His reply melted her heart. "I like burritos!" he said. After a significant time dating, they've been happily married for several years now.

As the years have gone by, Tala went from being fiercely independent around finances to getting comfortable with leaving her investment banking career to become a "starving artist" and having Jacob support them both. Being in a relationship where they are working toward the same goals as a couple seems to have removed the need Tala felt to assert her fierce financial independence that partially contributed to her failed previous marriage.

››› *Julie and Alex Bradford*

Julie and Alex Bradford are both entrepreneurs, each owning a separate business with its accompanying bank account. They also have separate personal bank accounts that are each funded with income from their businesses. Even before they started their businesses, they kept their bank accounts and income separate. They didn't intentionally design a system for their joint finances, but one evolved organically that worked for them. Given their separate businesses, combining their finances was never a consideration. They have equal ownership of their family residence, so Alex pays their mortgage and Julie pays the bills related to the house, such as utilities, property tax, housekeeping, and minor repairs. Julie says it "comes out about even," based on their income and the amount they each have after paying their part of the family bills, and that's close enough for them. They each buy and pay for the cars they drive and any accompanying expenses. If business is slow for one or the other, the other one "picks up the slack," as Julie describes it. As their kids were growing up, Julie paid for their private school and Alex set aside money for their future college. He paid for supplemental activities and she bought their clothes.

Julie shares with me that as a teenager, she vowed that she would never be controlled financially by a man. She watched her father, a first-generation immigrant from a culture where men were "in charge," make all decisions about how money would be spent in their family. Throughout her childhood, she observed the effect her father's dominance had on her mother. Julie and Alex didn't plan the details of how their expenses would be divided. They discussed Julie's commitment to handling her own money and not being controlled by a man, and this understanding helped a process evolve that works well for both of them. Over the years, they discussed each issue as it came, and their splitting the costs by category worked out to be even enough for them to be comfortable.

Julie says, "The downside is there is not much communication about money, and we have not really 'become one' as a married couple by combining our money. But it works for us!" I would add that their strategy for handling money as a couple flowed from their personal values that were clearly stated. Even as a teenager, Julie was aware of her feelings around the way finances were handled between her parents. She made a decision not to follow in her mother's footsteps as a wife. Julie shares with me that she and Alex have never had an argument about money.

The Bradfords' situation is somewhat unique in that they both own separate businesses, and therefore, keeping their money separate when they first got together happened organically rather than by design. As they bought their first home and their family grew so that they needed to provide for their children, they continued using the money habits that worked for them. Julie told me that with hindsight, she wishes she and Alex had talked more about how they would handle their money, but given how well their system works for them, she understands why they didn't. As we'll see next with Nate and Carrie, the Bradfords' way of handling finances doesn't work for everybody.

››› *Nate and Carrie*

As a dual-working couple, Nate and Carrie put equal amounts into a joint account at the beginning of each month. This account was used for expenses related to their home and their son, Justin. Carrie's parents had bought her a townhouse while she was in college, and over several years of graduate school and working, she parlayed that townhouse into the ability to buy the home she shared with Nate without needing a mortgage. Their joint account covered utilities, minor repairs, property taxes, and other shared family expenses.

Talking about money was always painful for Nate and Carrie, so they avoided the topic as much as possible. They came from significantly different backgrounds and weren't as comfortable with things being "about even" as Julie and Alex. So tracking the exact cost of items was more important to them than it was to the Bradfords. This required a considerable amount of time and transferring of money between accounts to keep everything equal when one of them paid for joint expenses from their individual account. It was important to both of them to have this level of accuracy as to who paid for what, and therefore this part of their process worked for them. Carrie told me that their exact accounting worked pretty well when things were simpler, but it might have been helpful if they'd adapted their methods over time as their family life became more complex.

What didn't work was the resentment Carrie felt around being the one who took responsibility for keeping track of the amount in the joint account. Often, the designated amount they each contributed on the first of the month wasn't enough to pay for all the purchases they made. As Carrie tracked the bank balance, she advised Nate when it was low or overdrawn so they both needed to add more funds. But Nate habitually delayed putting his share into the account. Therefore, Carrie identified her process as "nagging" Nate, which created stress in their relationship. Ultimately, she refused to put her money into the account until he had deposited his because he often lost track of the amount he needed to add and assumed she would cover his part. As I worked with Carrie, who felt a significant burden of responsibility around their family finances, I suggested some strategies to help remove her stress. These improved some of the logistical issues, but ultimately, their differences in handling money became a factor in their decision to separate as a couple.

››› *Jonathan and Marianne*

Other couples, like Jonathan and Marianne, continue to use the methods they learned from their parents. Fortunately for them, each set of parents handled money similarly, using a single joint checking account shared by both partners. This often happens when a couple has a single income or significantly different levels of income. Jonathan and Marianne mirrored their parents' situations by each putting their total salary into a joint account, with all expenses being paid from it.

In their case, Marianne earns significantly more money than Jonathan, but he spends large amounts on what she calls his "toys." They rarely talk about purchases before making them, and the appearance of a new car in the driveway infuriated Marianne. While having a single joint bank account can be a useful strategy, I've seen it create the most discord of all the methods, especially when communication around money and purchases doesn't flow easily. Fairness can become a divisive issue, especially in situations where one partner perceives the other's spending as excessive. Marianne bristles as she tells me that her income affords Jonathan the luxuries he buys.

››› *Mitch and Meagan*

Conflict can also result from a difference between reality and perception, as often happens with Mitch and Meagan. Mother to a family of five children, with kids ranging from early teenagers to adults in their late twenties, Meagan earns a teacher's salary and does all the shopping for their family. Mitch is an entrepreneur with a good salary. They share a joint checking account, each depositing their income into it.

Every month when Mitch gets the credit card statement that is in his name, he "flips his lid," as Meagan describes his outbursts. He takes Meagan to task for spending too much on the children's clothes, on eating out when they could eat at home, on gifts for their grandchildren, and pretty much everything she buys. While it's probable that Meagan could spend less, she's buying for a large family. It's also probable that they're both right: A family of seven costs a lot of money, but it also might not need to cost as much as Meagan spends. Regardless of who's "right," Mitch and Meagan have significant conflict over money that damages their marriage.

››› *Carl and Carol*

For Carl and Carol Johnson, combining their income has a different outcome. Married for more than fifty years, they have always combined their money. They've held a monthly financial meeting since they were newlyweds. As their young family grew to five members, Carl provided the sole income, and Carol managed their home and the family finances. After their youngest started school, Carol embarked on a lucrative real estate career. Still, she managed the finances and they continued

> their monthly meetings so they both knew where they stood financially. Today, they are retired and living on his pension and investments they made from Carol's real estate income. The difference between these two couples is that the Johnsons established a pattern of communicating about money early in their marriage. There's no stress or misunderstanding because they've always discussed their finances, made joint decisions about spending, and shared knowledge about their available funds. They enjoy making purchasing decisions together for big and small items alike. They communicate about money in a way that has served them well.

As we can see, these couples have significantly different methods of dealing with joint finances, and most of them work, at least for a time, some better than others. For those that don't work as well, a lack of communication creates more conflict than the specific way they share finances. Rather than considering that a particular methodology is "right" or "wrong," using one that allows couples to achieve their goals without creating stress or disharmony is important. Talking about emotions around who makes financial decisions, and what is decided, goes a long way toward financial security and avoiding conflict.

I encourage you to keep in mind that the timing and setting for talking about money often affect the outcome of the discussion. Some couples will want to schedule a preset time to talk about finances, maybe on a weekly or monthly basis like the Johnsons. When I returned to college at the age of forty, with two kids at home and precious little time for conversations with Kent, we cherished our Saturday morning "dates." We commandeered "our table" at a favorite coffee shop nearly every Saturday morning for four years. We typically arrived around 7 a.m. to be sure we got the table we wanted, and we were often still there when the lunch crowd started arriving. It became a ritual that we held sacred. We took advantage of this time to discuss all that had happened during the previous week, which included family finances.

The beauty of stories is that we can take bits and pieces of each that encourage our reflection and ignore whatever doesn't fit. You might want to consider your own ideas about money before discussing them with your partner. Maybe you think you know their thoughts, but this is a great opportunity to test your assumptions while engaging in a deeper conversation. Hopefully, the questions that follow will provide you with a starting point.

SOMETHING TO THINK ABOUT

- What are your thoughts on having combined or separate finances? Does your partner have similar or different ideas?
- What happens emotionally when you discuss finances with your partner/significant other?
- Do you dread talking with your partner about money? If so, why might that be?
- What financial issues are difficult to discuss?
- What issues do you consider off-limits?
- What goes unsaid that you'd like to discuss, but you don't?
- What would be your preferred method for handling finances with your partner?
- Who pays the bills, keeps track of balances, monitors your spending, and transfers funds when needed? Are you and your partner in agreement about these logistics?
- Can you and your partner identify arguments that are so repetitive that you could almost "argue by number"?
- How might you have better communication about your finances, i.e., scheduling a regular finance meeting together?
- What items might you want to include in your agenda for a monthly meeting?
- Which stories in this chapter would you like to discuss with your partner?

Chapter 15

Kids and Money

I've found that parents often find it difficult to provide their children with guidance about how to think about money. As a result, a few schools offer elective courses in financial literacy to better prepare students for adulthood. Without training from parents or schools, kids are expected to absorb the knowledge, information, and skills to manage finances through osmosis.

Many great books have been written about kids and money. Given that you can read books and articles that address teaching kids financial literacy, we won't cover that ground here. For our conversation, let's talk about the importance of having open communication about money. It's important to remember that our kids are picking up on our attitudes about money, just as we did from our parents, and they did from theirs.

We'd do well to keep in mind that discussing money with kids is not having "the talk," where we have one conversation and consider the subject covered once and for all. To be more effective, we need to have an ongoing dialogue where money is discussed in the same ways we discuss everyday family living. Furthermore, it's helpful to share with them the process by which decisions are made in our family, though they'll draw their own conclusions from watching us. We have multiple opportunities to teach our kids about money from the time they're quite young. In the same way we might discuss what's for dinner tonight, what family activities we are doing together this weekend, and the choices we make about any number of topics, we can incorporate conversations about money that let our kids know what we think and why. Given that this is likely different from how you were raised, you'll want to look for opportunities to include money in conversations.

You might wonder about the age to begin these conversations. I encourage you to keep in mind that your comments will be filtered through a child's mind and maturity. Still, when money is openly discussed as part of our family's everyday conversation, there's no age that is too young—as long as you're thoughtful about what you say to children of differing ages. And remember, it's never too late to start, so if you have teenagers and are wishing you'd started earlier, now is a great time to begin.

My Story

Comments about the lack of money in our family created my fear and scarcity mentality because of the ways Mom talked about it. Growing up with a single mom who was unprepared to take care of herself, let alone two little human beings, I lived in a household of scarcity mentality on steroids. Mom made nearly every decision throughout her life through the lens of, "How much will it cost?"—typically followed by, "We can't afford it."

As a young child, I knew more about money—or, more accurately, the lack thereof—than a young child was capable of processing. I think Mom used money to explain the many "why nots": why we couldn't have soft drinks or dessert or paper towels, why we couldn't go places with our friends, why we didn't go on vacations (and rarely to amusement parks) or have popcorn at the movie theater.

It's no wonder I vividly recall being about four years old when I heard a jingle on the car radio: "Need money? Dial DIAL for a loan," the announcer said. The numbers for DIAL would have been 3425 on an old rotary phone. I thought that one phone call could solve our money woes, as I asked, "Mommy, if we need money so badly, why don't we just dial DIAL for a loan?" Now, as an adult, I have no doubt that Mom's intention was to try to help us understand the limits of her ability to give us what we needed, as well as the message she left unsaid: that she would have liked to have been able to provide those things, but her meager income could only stretch enough to cover basic necessities.

Answering my question about the radio jingle, she explained to me at my young age how loans must be repaid, with interest, and how Mommy's income was insufficient to cover one more payment. So it was that I learned that money was what Mommy earned in order to put food on the table and a roof over our heads, but there was never enough for what she called "frills," like paper towels, Kleenex, soft drinks, or dessert.

As a child, I never considered that Grandma sewed all my clothes so Mom wouldn't have to buy them. But as an adult, I know beyond a shadow of a doubt that Grandma also loved sewing for me, even though she had a full-time job. Still, it's unlikely that she would have spent weekends and evenings sewing for me under different circumstances, especially after a long day of work.

Since I was a child before the days of credit cards, and Mom wouldn't "dial DIAL for a loan," getting money to make ends meet often meant going into debt at the National Bank of Grandma. In my eyes, Grandma's "wealth" was made evident by my being allowed to get pecan pie on Sundays when she and Grandad took me to the cafeteria after church. She let me choose anything on the serving line without considering the cost, but it was the pecan pie that delighted me most.

With Grandma's money came Grandma's opinions—or as Mom experienced it, Grandma's judgment—and it seems to me that Mom did everything within her power to avoid asking for another "loan." I now understand how calling it a loan allowed Mom to save face and gave Grandma a way to present it to Grandad without positioning it as yet another "gift." I wonder how much they discussed how they helped Mom throughout my childhood, or if they did whatever they did without talking about it.

Mom didn't talk overtly about the judgment she felt from Grandma, but I didn't need her words to understand the tension between them. Somehow, even at a young age, I knew that it was related to money. Its negativity often filled the room. If Grandma had to loan us money for food until Mom's next paycheck, then she thought she had a "right to her opinion" on other items Mom used her money to buy—at least, that was Mom's interpretation. The other messages were Mom's own "Voice of Judgment,"[1] which I imagine told her that she was inept at handling finances, that she was a disappointment to her mother, and that getting pregnant and having to drop out of school midway through tenth grade meant she couldn't earn a living wage to support her children. She probably felt guilty for marrying her middle school sweetheart at fifteen, and further berated herself because her children's father left the state to avoid paying child support for their two children.

What Grandma actually said, I'll never know. What matters is how I have seen my mom and my clients mold their beliefs about the scarcity—or abundance—of money into self-talk that greatly impacts their relationships with others, their own identity, their perceived happiness, and the messages they send their children.

Time demands on American parents take their toll in numerous ways. For many, time at home is maxed out from getting dinner ready after a stressful work day, reminding kids to practice their musical instruments and do their homework—or working with them on it—filling out approval forms for field trips, delivering kids to after-school activities, finishing work brought home from the office, planning next month's family events, coercing kids to go to bed, and sometimes working remotely from home, all while needing some "downtime" for themselves. The idea of having a specific conversation with their kids around money understandably takes a back seat to more pressing concerns.

On the other hand, if money has been regularly discussed as part of ongoing conversations, then it's not necessary to think about having time for special discussions. Furthermore, when we've been talking to our kids about money most of their lives, we avoid situations where the only time we talk about money is when there's a problem to be resolved.

Additionally, the extent to which kids are targeted by advertisers is almost impossible for parents to overcome. I mention this to provide you with an inkling of information that describes the magnitude of the issue but will leave it for you to further investigate. There's more information for parents on the internet than anyone has time to absorb, especially as it relates to screen time.

As evidenced by YouTube videos about how advertisements rewire kids' brains and the impact of junk food ads (98 percent of ads targeting kids are for junk food!), as well as a report by the American Psychological Association (APA) Task Force on Advertising and Children—which estimates that "advertisers spend more than $12 billion per year to reach the youth market" and that "children view more than 40,000 commercials each year"—our kids are being bombarded.[2] In the same report, though, the APA points out that advertisers have been targeting kids since long before radio, television, or the internet: "The British Parliament passed legislation in 1874 intended to protect children from the efforts of merchants to induce them to buy products and assume debt." So, this problem is not new and will never go away. In addition to being informed consumers, parents would do well to avail themselves of the many opportunities to learn techniques to help their children stay safe and be aware of the efforts of marketing tactics. One such resource is the YouTube video "Junk Food Ads and Kids" by Common Sense Media, which provides parents with strategies to counteract ads targeting their children.[3]

Now, let's look at some stories that will provide some insight into ways to work with kids around money.

››› *Oketa and Kalisia, Margene and Emily*

> Recently, I discussed our kids and money with my friends Oketa and Margene. Oketa told us that her daughter, Kalisia, is taking "financial literacy" as an elective in high school. After a class discussion on

interest rates, Kalisia and her mom talked about the purchase of their new home. This provided an opportunity for a discussion not only about interest rates, but also about home ownership and mortgages. Their natural conversation created more curiosity than sitting Kalisia down for a talk about money. It led to discussions about how Kalisia wanted more responsibility for her money, how credit cards work, and how debt affects the ability to buy a home.

Oketa told us Kalisia uses her money wisely and feels empowered by having money in her bank account. She told her mom she dislikes seeing her bank account balance drop because she has to earn more money to build it back up. Oketa, an accountant, insists that Kalisia keep track of where her money is spent.

As Oketa talked, Margene commented on how each of her three kids has a significantly different relationship with money. As she listened to Oketa describe Kalisia's enthusiasm for learning about finances, she was reminded how her thirty-five-year-old daughter, Emily, has never wanted to discuss money at any age. Regardless of how Margene broached the subject, Emily's "eyes glazed over." Margene remembered being puzzled when fiercely independent Emily commented that she would marry a man who would handle her finances. Ultimately, while Emily thought her husband handled their family finances, she learned after their divorce that many of their joint accounts had been sent to collection agencies. Consequently, she and her second husband make financial decisions together.

Margene also mentioned that Emily's older brother received a credit card offer when he was eighteen, unbeknown to his parents. He exhausted the credit limit and got into debt, starting his credit history on the wrong foot. Margene intercepted credit card offers before they reached her other two kids when they turned eighteen. Her older son worked to get out of debt, and as a result of his early experience, uses credit cards wisely today. Some people who get into credit card debt at a young age never get out. The book *The Debt Project: 99 Portraits Across America* by Brittany M. Powell describes the human stories of ninety-nine people for whom debt has severely impacted their lives.

››› *Sherry and Leslie*

Some kids remember their early experiences with money as "fun." Sherry tells me of the joy of having a passbook savings account as a kid. She reminisced about going to the bank with her dad to deposit $.50 in her account each week. As the teller recorded the deposit, she watched her balance grow. She described how she replicated the experience with her daughter, Leslie.

When I chatted with Leslie, a college student, she told me her own fond memories of her passbook savings account. She described how she worked through high school to help her unemployed single mom pay utility bills. She said the spending habits that started in childhood still serve her well. Even though student loans create anxiety, she appreciates that they are less than they would be if she weren't working forty hours a week. She sees that many of her classmates don't have the same work ethic she developed while watching her mom struggle financially.

⟫ *Heather*

When our daughter was a junior in college, the university credit union offered students a credit line to buy a new car. I suppose they were willing to take a risk that juniors would be able to pay their loans with income from their first jobs after graduation. Even though Heather had jobs during college and a checking account from the age of ten, she'd never had a credit card in her name, and therefore had no payment history that would have provided a credit score qualifying her for the $18,000 they loaned her to buy a brand-new car.

She continued working two jobs throughout the summer, from 9 a.m. to 9 p.m., with only breaks for meals and to go from one job to the other, so she could save enough to make all the payments that would be due during her senior year. Still, having a car loan caused her considerable anxiety as she worked while attending school. She paid off the balance earlier than the term of the loan, and she's avoided debt throughout her life, paying cash for every car since. I agree with Margene that kids are hardwired differently around money. I can't imagine that Heather will ever tolerate debt.

I feel for parents who meet resistance when trying to teach kids about money. For Oketa, it's an easy conversation with Kalisia, but Oketa describes learning about money "the hard way," without guidance from her parents. Furthermore, knowing how much to tell kids at what ages can be difficult. Kids like Emily who don't want to discuss money make it even harder for parents to broach the topic.

Raising well-adjusted kids who make wise, healthy money choices can be challenging. We typically want them to know how to manage their money by the time they leave home. Although each child is different, kids' understanding of money is impacted by the socioeconomic status (SES) of their parents. In my experience, helping kids become financially literate can be more difficult in wealthy families. When parents have the means to provide abundantly for their children, they often do so. It's natural to want to give our kids the things they want. For parents who have a significant amount of money, it can be easier to buy a solution to an immediate problem than to address the underlying issues.

Both affluent parents and those who struggle with money can teach our kids about priorities, values, responsibilities, needs vs. wants, saving, investing, and generosity. We can use shopping experiences to give them information about how we make decisions. We might share how we wish we'd made a different decision involving money. What's important is that we take advantage of teachable moments when they present themselves.

››› *Ryan, Lauren, and Kaleigh*

Ryan and Lauren included their five-year-old daughter, Kaleigh, in a family discussion about sharing with others. As they discussed their family's charitable giving, they used language appropriate for Kaleigh's age, like donating to people "who take care of pets" or "give food to hungry children." Ryan asked Kaleigh who she'd like to help. She'd seen a TV commercial about hungry children in a third-world country and asked if they could send them money. She had been listening as her parents talked about their family values and ways to make a difference in the world. Perhaps that experience was the genesis of her service in the Peace Corps.

Sometimes siblings' approaches to money are so different as to make one wonder how they grew up with the same parents. Kids exhibit preconceived notions about money from a young age. Some seem to have been born to be spenders, while others prefer saving, regardless of outside influence. Some will always have money, while others never seem to have enough to meet their basic needs, as we see next with the Williams family.

››› *The Williams Family*

The three teenaged Williams boys differ in their relationships with money. Michael, thirteen, takes after his mother, spending whatever he has and running out of money before the end of every week. Sixteen-year-old Mark spends frugally, watching his bank account grow, and Max, seventeen, gets what he needs, checking his bank balance daily. The kids get equal amounts of allowance on Friday, but

> their bank balances on Thursday nights range from Michael having close to zero, Max having about $500, to Mark having over $1,000. Their parents, Marti and Ben, have been surprised watching their three sons manage money so differently.
>
> However our kids are hardwired, they need to know how money and our family values coincide. This can happen through spur-of-the-moment comments as well as in-depth conversations. As parents, we need to think about the messages we want to convey. To do this, we need to know what we think about money. For example, Marti and Ben want their sons to have a basic understanding of what things cost and to understand cost vs. value. When the boys were younger, the couple made sacrifices that the boys were too young to understand, ones that resulted in the family's current affluence. They want their sons to know that their lifestyle came at a price. They want to ensure that their kids don't grow up with a sense of entitlement but instead have the satisfaction that comes from doing a job well and contributing to society.

Regardless of a family's wealth, there will always be other kids who are able to have and do more than ours. This can result from differences in values more than affordability. When our kids see that our family doesn't spend money like their friends—even when we could afford to—we need to help them understand that our choices come from our values. We want to teach them to be informed consumers and to know what's needed to be financially secure.

Most parents want their kids to handle money responsibly by the time they leave home. Whether they go to college or launch directly into the workforce, they need to be financially independent. These are a few of the wishes I've heard from parents:

- We want them to have a sense of value and to know what things cost.
- We have an affluent lifestyle, so we want them to understand what it took for us to accomplish financial success.
- They will one day have a sizable inheritance, so we want them to be prepared to use it wisely, and for it not to discourage them from working toward a satisfying life.
- We don't want the quality of their lives to be thwarted because they spend everything they get or get themselves into debt.
- We don't want them to do without because they're afraid to spend the money they have available.
- We want them to understand how school loans work.
- We want them to know the importance of retirement planning.
- We want them to be informed consumers.
- We want them to know how to be financially successful, whatever their dreams might be.

As they transition away from living at home, kids face a significant learning curve in many aspects of their lives, from independently managing their time to navigating boundless choices around making new friends, eating junk food or healthy food, partying all night or getting a good night's rest, personal fitness, and spending. When they've learned about money throughout childhood, they don't have to add financial literacy to that learning curve. It's helpful to remember that teaching kids about money is like teaching them to drive a car. They're going to make mistakes, and we hope those mistakes result in a fender-bender rather than a major accident. It is our responsibility to prepare them as much as possible for whatever the future holds.

››› *Heather and Charles*

As I previously mentioned, our daughter, Heather, had her first checking account at the age of ten. We deposited a consistent monthly allowance and were involved in her choices about how to spend her money. At that age, we helped her write checks, but we were doing the thinking. Over time, she was given more opportunities to decide what she would pay for. She covered the bills for riding lessons and horse shows. As a result, she was comfortable with money when she went to college. After she got there, she became sick and lost track of her finances, causing her to have insufficient funds to cover a check to a pharmacy. She was distraught as she told me what she'd done, but it never happened again.

With Heather being ten years older than her brother, we used her success with money to prepare Charles to handle his own. When he was in sixth grade, I tracked our spending on items bought specifically for him to determine a monthly amount he would need. I divided the annual cost of purchases by twelve to set his monthly allowance. This would require him to plan for the months when his spending needs would be greater than his monthly allowance, like at the beginning of the school year, when he'd need to pay for school fees, supplies, and new clothes.

After he'd been handling his money for a few months, Charles outgrew his dress shoes, needing to buy a man's size for the first time. His choices were limited to two styles in the men's size six—one that was not age-appropriate and the other, Italian leather loafers, which he immediately wanted. I reminded him that the cost would use most of his monthly allowance and the shoes wouldn't fit for long, as his feet were still growing. Still, the decision was his. Within a few months, when the shoes became too small, he bought another pair of the same style in a larger size. To this day, he knows what he likes and makes sacrifices to get what's important to him.

You might be surprised to learn that some of my teenage clients don't like to spend money. Similar to Gail's story in Chapter Six, some kids prefer to watch their balances grow, so they'd rather do without things. As parents, we need to help these kids become comfortable with spending. How to accomplish this will vary with the personality of your children and your relationship with them. Again, the internet provides copious amounts of information that will help you determine which strategies to have in your tool kit. You'll likely need to try different ones for different situations and adjust them over time.

You might be thinking that reluctance to spend money wouldn't be your child's issue. When Ben Williams, dad to Michael, Mark, and Max, determined the items their sons would buy with their money, he was reluctant to include clothes. He said they'd rather wear pants with holes in them than buy new ones, so to avoid a confrontation, he left clothes off the list. He believed that if he asked them to use their own money, they'd never have new clothes. So, we strategized together to identify other spending categories and decided they like shoes, so they would pay for their footwear, as well as haircuts, personal entertainment, and meals with friends.

The process for handling money changes as kids' ages change, but they learn from each experience. Start with an amount of money large enough so they can make some less-than-desirable choices and learn from their "mistakes," but not so much that they can do significant damage. By the time they leave home, they will have the tools they need to be financially successful, regardless of the amount of money they have.

One other issue I see often has to do with requiring kids to work or do chores to earn their allowance. Obviously, this is a personal decision, but I recommend that children receive an allowance without being told they are earning it. This sends the message that they're participating in the family by receiving a share of the family income. When you expect them to contribute to family life in whatever way you want them to be involved, tying their household services to money undermines the message that you're all doing your part for the welfare of the family. In the same way that an employer doesn't deduct from your paycheck when you forget to do something or miss a deadline, the lessons to be learned from separating finances from discipline will serve your children well.

Most importantly, we want our kids to have a roadmap to financial wellness and to see money as a tool they can use to get what's important to them, whether that's things or experiences. By talking with them about money throughout their lives, they'll go into their significant relationships assuming their partner has similar experiences, and if their partner doesn't, perhaps they'll have the tools to teach them.

SOMETHING TO THINK ABOUT

Below are some questions I use directly with kids to understand their ideas around money. I've also provided questions for parents to help you think about how you'd like to help your kids be better prepared to handle money. You might want to discuss these questions with your child's other parent to determine whether you agree before using them to guide your next steps. I hope you'll use these questions as a starting place and invite you to add your own questions.

For Kids

- What does having or not having money mean to you?
- How do you spend your money?
- How much is a lot of money?
- How much money would you like to *earn* some day?
- How much money would you like to *have* some day?
- What are some ways you could get that amount of money?
- What does "manage your money" mean to you?
- What are some examples of wise choices you've made about spending money?
- What are some choices around spending that you wish you'd made differently?
- Would you rather spend your money or save it?
- If you'd like to save money, how much would you like to have?

- What are your thoughts around giving money to other people or charitable organizations?
- How much allowance would you like to receive? Would you rather receive your allowance weekly or monthly?
- What differences do you see in the ways your dad and mom make decisions about how money is spent?

For Parents

- What is important for your child to know about money at this time in their life?
- What is important for your child to know about money between now and when they leave home?
- What are you doing to prepare your child to be financially literate by the time they leave home?
- What have you done with your child to teach them about money?
- How does your child get what they want or need (e.g., school clothes, concert tickets, fun items)? For example, do they ask and get it? Do they pay with their allowance?
- Does your child get most of what they ask for?
- How often do you think your child should get "paid"? Weekly? Monthly?
- How much do you think is a reasonable amount per month for allowance?
- How much money should they get monthly over and above the amount you/they think they need?
- What should happen if your child runs out of money before the next payment they're scheduled to receive?

- Do you think you should provide a car for your child? If so, at what age?
- Do you think you should pay for your child's college expenses? If so, all? Some? Which ones? How much?
- Do you expect your child to earn money before they leave home? If so, what items will they be expected to buy with money they earn?
- Do you and your partner/spouse agree on what your child needs to know about money?
- Do you agree on how much money your child should have available to spend?
- How is a decision made when you disagree?
- What are your values around money that are important for your child to know? How are you teaching your child those values?

Chapter 16

Families and Money

In this chapter, we'll look at ways families deal with money. Family practices around money can be supportive and advantageous, but they can also be fraught with confusion, conflict, and turmoil. We grow up with subliminal messages about family traditions and taboos that can convey belonging to our families. Money can create havoc with relationships within families, often exacerbated by adult members having substantially different incomes, assets, spending habits, or ideas about money. To belong, we believe we must adhere to unspoken family practices around money—which were rarely stated overtly.

Unspoken rules around loans between family members often create the most havoc. For example, is it expected that: (1) money will be loaned between family members, (2) we don't loan money to family members, or (3) we don't loan money to *specific* family members? Do family members have a common understanding of what "borrowing" means within the family? Is it clear to both parties that the exchange is truly meant to be a loan? Or is money loaned with an unspoken understanding that it isn't expected to be repaid—or that both parties know it is unlikely that it will be repaid? In my family, a "loan" implied repayment by virtue of what it was called, but it was done without documentation or terms of repayment. Based on experience of previous unpaid loans, both parties inherently agreed on nonrepayment. Therefore, I advise clients not to give money under the guise of a loan without documented terms and a stated expectation of repayment. If they don't believe they'll be repaid, I suggest they give the money as a clearly stated gift or not give it at all.

On the other hand, money can be loaned successfully to family members when handled with professionalism, honesty, and integrity, as Margaret's family reveals.

››› *Margaret*

> Margaret loaned money to each of her four adult children without creating problems. She became a wealthy widow in her early fifties. As her kids matured, she made them loans that allowed them to buy their first homes. These loans included signed promissory notes with repayment details and interest. As their families grew and they moved to larger homes, they used proceeds from the sale of their first homes to pay the loans in full. Margaret loaned them additional funds to buy larger homes. Because the family had a healthy communication process and her kids knew they were expected to repay their loans, Margaret never worried about repayment and was never disappointed. She took

great joy in providing the money that helped her kids and grandchildren live in nice homes.

Families can go sideways over money in some bizarre ways. For example, I broke an unspoken family rule that possessions were never sold to family members; they were to be gifted. When I mentioned to my mom that I had posted a bedroom suite on the internet to sell, she said she'd like to have it and asked the price. For years after she bought it, she made subtle comments that conveyed how she didn't appreciate that I'd accepted the money she offered.

Families can also become conflicted around payments for services between family members. As we'll see with Dennis and Dolores and their daughters, Mary and Celeste, the benefits of an open dialogue about expectations around money outweigh the cost of the discomfort that might be experienced from discussing the arrangement in advance.

››› *Dennis and Dolores, Mary and Celeste*

Dennis and Dolores Thompson, part of the Greatest Generation, lived into their nineties. Dennis handled the family's finances, but as he got older, he had neither the energy nor the mental acuity to continue. His stress over forgotten payments sent him to the emergency room because he thought he was having a heart attack.

Their daughter, Mary, who had recently left a position as an accountant, offered to help her parents get control of their finances. Mary spent eighteen months putting her parents' complex financial affairs in order. She included Dennis as she set up online payments and color-coded systems so he knew what was happening with their money. Over time, his memory deteriorated, making her efforts more difficult.

What started as an offer to help her parents have control of their finances became more time-consuming than Mary had time to devote. Therefore, she suggested that they hire someone to handle the financial activities. Her parents told her they wouldn't trust a stranger to be involved with their money and asked her to continue doing the work. Having watched her dad's decline, she didn't have the heart to tell them she wouldn't continue. Given that she'd previously been paid a salary for similar work, she hoped they would offer to pay her, but she said nothing about it. She knew they could afford to pay her and that money was not an acceptable topic of conversation in their family.

Mary continued spending several days a month helping her parents, with resentment building around not being compensated for her time. Ultimately, she returned to a full-time accounting position where she would be appropriately paid for similar work. When she told her parents she couldn't continue because she was working, they agreed to let her find a paid accountant to do the work she'd been doing for the previous five years.

After Dennis died, Mary's unmarried and unemployed sister, Celeste, left her home in another state for extended periods of time to manage their mother's in-home caregivers. She established terms under which she would work, including time and money. Dolores agreed to pay Celeste the requested

> amount, apparently without considering that Mary had provided services to their parents without compensation.
>
> The Thompsons' story reminds us of the importance of talking about money, even in families where the topic is considered off-limits for discussion. While Mary resented not being compensated, the fear of discussing money with her parents overrode her need to be paid for her time. Yet, when her sister clearly stated her financial requirements, Dolores seemed to have no problem agreeing to Celeste's request. Mary's resentment turned to hurt feelings that have not been repaired, even after Dolores's death.

Additionally, when dealing with aging parents, it's helpful to know our family histories. If Grandpa lived with you as a kid, you likely learned that your family takes care of their elders. If your grandparents lived in a retirement home, you might reasonably assume your parents will do the same. And, if your grandparents lived in a nursing home with your family visiting only on major holidays or not at all, that is your model. Regardless of the model, families benefit from discussing expectations around finances and caregiving. They might discover that the way things were done in previous generations looks different at a different point in time and under different circumstances.

Another issue many American families face occurs when young adult children reach an age where they are expected to move out of their parents' homes. As we've seen in recent times, this transition sometimes doesn't go as planned. When adult children live with their parents because they can't afford to move to their own homes, communication about the financial issues of living together becomes essential to maintaining a good relationship. The Williams family, whom we met in Chapter Fifteen, provides an example of working through some potential problems before they happen and the benefits of having a plan for dealing with unexpected things as they come up.

))) *Max and Marti*

One of the Williams boys, Max, went to trade school after high school but needed to live at home until he finished his training and got a job. He'd been living with his dad as he finished high school, but his trade school was closer to his mom's house. Max and his mom, Marti, knew from previous experience that they might have challenges living together. They asked me to create a document that could provide guidance as they ran into issues they thought might derail their living happily together. We discussed their anticipated stumbling blocks, and I suggested ways they could plan for those situations. They established the length of time Max would live with Marti. The three of us discussed my recommendations and made some tweaks, and they both signed a document that established details of their agreement.

They also mutually decided on an amount that Max would pay for joint living expenses from his part-time job. A few months later, when he needed to change jobs, he had another job the day after quitting the first one. Had he not made the commitment to cover his part of the living expenses, it's possible that he wouldn't have been as motivated to get another job so quickly. When

> the time allotted for Marti and Max to live together needed to be extended, their initial agreement allowed them to adjust the end date.
>
> Plans can be changed as life changes, but much is to be gained from having thought about the issues before they happen. Since Max is the oldest of three sons, his brothers have the benefit of watching how he and their mother manage the process of his living at home as a young adult. If they find themselves needing a similar accommodation, their mother and brother have provided a healthy role model.

Yet another scenario involves aging parents struggling to help their adult children financially in ways that work well for everyone. Several of my clients had similar situations, which were the catalyst for engaging me to help with their financial matters. In two of the families, giving money to support their adult children negatively impacted their own financial well-being. As the adult children were providing for their own families, it was obvious to me that their parents felt a responsibility to provide for their grandchildren, whereas I can only surmise how they might have made different choices for an adult child without a family.

I've also seen the reverse: adult children helping aging parents who don't have adequate retirement funds to meet their financial needs. These clients struggle to balance their ability to provide for their own family's needs while also considering ways to help their parents. As the adult children are typically at their peak earning age, they sometimes have to choose between providing some of the niceties of life for their children that their income affords and helping their parents with living expenses. In other cases, parents observe their adult kids having what they believe is "more than enough" and want them to provide some of the same luxuries for themselves. Sometimes, they add a layer of guilt, communicating that the adult child owes them for the care they provided them as children. I'll share a few more examples.

››› *Jan and Scott*

Through a series of unfortunate financial decisions, Jan—a widowed mother of four adult children with a dozen grandchildren—eventually exhausted her invested inheritance, having only Social Security to live on. When we started working together twenty years earlier, she thought she was financially set for life. As we saw in Chapter Twelve, her self-diagnosed ADD caused her to struggle with the logistics of paying bills, and she had no training to understand basic financial concepts. She didn't realize she'd given tens of thousands of dollars a year to help her eldest child, Scott, so he could pay rent and other living expenses for his large family. When we first started working together and I calculated the amount she'd sent to Scott in just the previous year alone, she was surprised it was in excess of $30,000. She told me she'd been sending Scott comparable amounts for many years, as well as giving lesser amounts to some of her other children. Looking at her total assets, it was clear that her generosity wasn't sustainable. She immediately made a difficult call to let Scott know she would not continue sending money.

Scott didn't like asking his aging mother for money any more than she liked refusing to send it. Since her decision, Jan has given Scott birthday money but has maintained her resolve to not send money for his family's living expenses. His wife and older teenage children now work to help support the household income.

Jan's situation might cause you to wonder how her decisions resulted in running out of money. It seems to me that nobody thinks it can happen to them. But it not only can—it does. Before Jan's husband died, his family business's office handled their personal finances for nearly all the years of their marriage. Jan got a monthly allowance to take care of the household needs. Therefore, she never learned how to handle money beyond one month of "spending money" at a time and knew nothing about paying bills. When her husband died unexpectedly just before his fiftieth birthday, leaving her to fend for herself with no one to guide her, she thought she had enough money to spend whatever she wanted for the rest of her life. It was not to be.

Besides the money that Jan gave to Scott's family, she took her large family on international trips. She custom-built an impressive house in the most affluent part of town. She moved often, buying and selling homes every few years, often at a financial loss. She withdrew from her investments to cover her rather lavish lifestyle until they were depleted so that the annual earnings couldn't keep up with her spending, and she exhausted the principal.

In the next example, we'll see another family whose efforts to provide financial assistance to their son created an unsustainable situation for their own financial well-being.

››› *The Taylor Family*

The Taylors, whom we met in Chapter Seven, had three grown sons. In our first meeting, Harold and Helen told me how their son Larry struggled with alcoholism but was turning his life around. They'd given a home to Larry and his family so they knew his family would always have a roof over their heads. They also helped him financially so that he could focus on finishing trade school without having to work. They expected to continue sending him money until he graduated, knowing he'd then be able to provide for his family. They never discussed between themselves or with Larry whether they expected the money they'd provided to be repaid, but when I asked, they acknowledged that they assumed it never would be.

The Taylors were spending money they didn't have to support Larry and his family. I was able to help them understand that they couldn't continue giving money to Larry and still be financially secure in their own future. I reminded them how they'd generously given him the equity in their previous home and paid the house payments while he was in school. They were able to let that be enough when they saw how helping Larry would negatively impact their ability to be financially independent for the rest of their lives.

Sometimes family dynamics around money result from differences in cultural traditions. In some families, grandparents came to the United States with their adult children to care for their grandchildren. In others, children bring their older parents from other countries so they can be together and to take care of them. Still other people came to the United States for college and are working to be able to one day bring their parents to share in their American way of life. Some establish themselves and then sponsor extended family members. And the children of some who came through Ellis Island generations ago still honor their parents' traditions by taking care of their families, whether parents or children.

Further, many factors impact financial experiences—from natural disasters that destroy entire communities to unexpected accidents that create sudden disabilities, to unforeseen environmental catastrophes, economic recessions, market reversals, and wars. Having lived in California for thirty years, I've had friends who fled raging fires with only the clothes on their backs and returned to the charred ruins of their homes and businesses. The same is true for the devastation caused by tornadoes, as my mom's house in Oklahoma was within blocks of being directly hit more than once. Here in Hawaii, when the Red Hill Naval Fuel Storage Facility leaked, more than three thousand families were forced from their homes for months because they couldn't drink, shower, or brush their teeth with tainted water from their taps. And speaking of brushing teeth, I'm reminded how my own life changed in the blink of an eye when I broke both ankles at the same time, resulting in being bedridden for weeks and unable to get to the bathroom sink to brush my teeth. You likely have other examples of unexpected events that drastically changed lives. As a result of these changes, lives are turned upside down as families experience upheaval, which sometimes includes becoming a "have not" overnight.

Still another issue that weighs heavily on some families centers around paying taxes. In the next stories, we'll see how tax payments seem to take on a life of their own, as they can create emotional stress in ways nothing else does. Let's take a look at why that is.

››› *John and Isabella*

John and Isabella are both self-employed, each owning different businesses but filing their taxes jointly. Consequently, they both owe quarterly tax estimates. Their differing sensitivities create more tension around tax payments than other topics. Philosophically and in practice, John spends while Isabella saves. With regard to taxes, John complains about the government "using his money" and therefore doesn't pay estimated taxes throughout the year. This creates significant anxiety for Isabella, who has intense fear of the IRS based on her childhood experience. When her family business–owning parents failed to submit payroll taxes that had been withheld from their employees' paychecks, the IRS "lowered the boom," as her mother described those difficult times when Isabella was a teenager. The IRS determined an amount her parents would have available for living expenses and took the remainder of their income from their bank account on a weekly basis. To this day, Isabella relives the fear any time the payment of taxes is discussed. Year after year, John and Isabella argue when quarterly tax payments are due, with Isabella wanting to pay them and John refusing. The arguments become even more heated when their annual tax returns reveal the amount they pay in penalties and interest for not having paid the estimated tax when it was due.

››› *Janie*

Janie is also required to pay tax estimates and tells me it bothers her to owe taxes at year-end. Unlike John in the previous story, she has no objection to the IRS using her money. She will happily pay an excess amount throughout the year to avoid a year-end payment on April 15th. As we discussed why she feels strongly about this, she said owing taxes at year-end feels like the "loss of her nest egg, plus the insult of having to pay taxes." Throughout her salaried career, Janie took pride in managing her withholding by claiming fewer dependents so that she got a sizable refund at year-end—what she calls her "nest egg." Intellectually, she knows she could put the same amount of money she had withheld into an account that earns interest to be used to pay the tax that is owed at year-end. Still, emotionally, she enjoyed using her tax refund as a way to treat herself to an annual special purchase. In her mind, because it was a reward for being financially responsible, the opposite—owing taxes—feels irresponsible to her.

These examples barely scratch the surface of topics that cause financial angst within families, but they hopefully trigger memories to uncover some of yours. Consider making a list to help you understand your relationship with your money. You might include:

- unspoken rules within families
- transferring money and possessions between family members
- loans vs. gifts
- payment for services within families
- caring for elderly relatives
- young adults living at home
- aging parents financially helping adult children
- exhausting financial resources before death
- honoring cultural traditions
- stress created by specific issues, e.g., tax payments

Timing Matters

Having worked with a number of octogenarians, nonagenarians, and one centenarian who were children during the Great Depression, I've seen how their childhood experiences around money have influenced their relationship with it. One might think that these children who also lived through the economic expansion of the 1950s and 1960s would have overcome the trauma they had as children of the 1930s, but often, they did not.

Trauma from their early years often impacts spending habits among the Greatest Generation. For example, those with limited money and space tend to buy large quantities with each grocery store visit. When I ask why they buy more than they have room to store, they can't tell me, but their age is the common thread: They were children during the Depression and lived with rationing during World War II. Many decades later, they buy more than necessary, as if they don't know if they will be able to get more when their supply runs out.

Given that the generation of children who grew up during the Depression is rapidly dwindling, how are their experiences still apparent today? Baby boomers were often children of a generation that lived with scarcity—their values likely served as a model that continued through subsequent generations. As we've discussed, it's not unusual for beliefs to be transferred to future generations without thought as to the beliefs' origins. A legend sometimes called "The Pot Roast Story" provides an example:

The Pot Roast Story

A young bride, whom we'll call Kayla, watched as her mother, Linda, prepared a pot roast for the family to enjoy. As Kayla watched Linda season the roast and put it in the pan, she asked, "Mom, why do you do that?" Linda, not knowing what she referred to as "that," asked what she meant. Kayla said, "You always cut a sliver of roast and set it to the side as you put it in the pan." Linda said she didn't know why, but her mother did it that way. When Linda later asked her mother, Betty, why she cut the roast into two pieces, Betty replied, "My pan was too small for the whole roast to fit in one piece, so I cut a sliver and wedged it into the side of my pan to make it fit."

Sometimes we don't know why we do what we do, but it's happened for generations within our families, so it's known and feels safe. But times change, and what was important for one generation may not work for the next. When we continue the patterns of our parents without question, we may end up living by rules that worked for their generation but do not work for us. To sort through what is ours and what's been passed to us without considering its value to us, we must be open to investigation and willing to process pain or trauma to move toward a healthier relationship with our money.

As we'll see in the following example, timing has an impact on other generations, as well. Studies are being done on millennials (those born between 1981 and 1996), and we have yet to see how Covid-19 will affect another generation of children.

››› *Liam and Oliver*

> Liam, a Silicon Valley entrepreneurial millennial, makes more money in a year than his parents made in a lifetime, which has allowed him to become a "have" after growing up as a "have not" in his parents' home. On the other hand, his friend Oliver follows national averages, having grown up in a financially secure home but now finding himself struggling financially as part of the first generation that may not achieve a life that is financially better than their parents.
>
> Studies show a dramatic increase in the number of millennials who are financially less successful than their parents, a number that has been trending upward for decades. *The Washington Post* reported in 2019 in an article titled "The Average Millennial Has a Net Worth of $8,000. That's Far Less Than Previous Generations":

> Millennials are doing far worse financially than generations before them, with student loans, rising rents and higher health-care costs pushing the average net worth below $8,000, a new study shows. The net worth of Americans aged 18 to 35 has dropped 34 percent since 1996, according to research released Thursday by Deloitte, the accounting and professional services giant. This demographic is paying more for education and such basics as food and transportation while incomes have largely flatlined.[1]

When our circumstances shift dramatically from the past, it's only natural to change how we approach spending and thinking about money to adjust to our current circumstances. However, this isn't always the case. Some who experience significant downturns in net worth will acknowledge how their financial status has changed and use earlier experiences to inform current decisions. Others, however, might not acknowledge that this shift has occurred, continuing to make choices from an emotional place their income does not support. In some cases, this inability to confront change has devastating repercussions when earlier changes in spending habits might have made the difference between long-term financial stability and financial devastation.

Furthermore, much has been written about millennials who came of age as the economy collapsed during the Great Recession of 2008. Many who face crushing student loan debt have adjusted their lifestyles to accommodate their financial situation. A Pew Research article titled "Millennial Life: How

Young Adulthood Today Compares with Prior Generations"[2] describes how millennials:

- are delaying or forgoing marriage
- are somewhat slower to form their own households
- are more likely to live at home with parents, and for a longer period of time
- are better educated than their grandparents
- have accumulated less wealth than same-age members of prior generations
- change locations significantly less than previous generations
- start families later

The societal implications of these factors will be studied by generations of sociologists to come. My son is one of these millennials, with an MBA and exceptional people skills. In spite of all these issues, he describes his generation as optimistic, adventurous, risk-tolerant, and aware of how quickly things can change. I agree with him, as my experience with his generation gives me enormous confidence that our future is in good hands. Even though they may not earn as much money or accumulate a comparable amount of net worth as their parents did at their age, they tend to focus on meaningful aspects of a good quality of life that allows them to have better relationships with others, as well as with themselves.

SOMETHING TO THINK ABOUT

- What, if any, are your childhood memories about how money was handled between family members?
- If you are aware of loans between family members, do you know if they were repaid? If not, what did you hear about the family member(s) who owed money?
- How would you feel about asking a family member for financial help?
- Do you and your partner have similar ideas about lending or giving your families financial help?
- If someone in your family provides professional services to you or other family members, do they receive payment? If not, how were the arrangements made, and do you know how that person feels about not being paid?
- In what ways does thinking about the payment of taxes affect you?
- What familial patterns around money came from earlier generations?
- If you have experienced significant financial changes over time, what are some ways those changes impact your way of thinking about money?
- If you're a millennial, how does your financial situation compare with your parents?
- If you're a millennial, what adjustments have you made because of when you were born?

Chapter 17

Dying and Money

Another area where people get tangled up around money is in deciding what will happen after they die. Furthermore, family dynamics can go haywire with expectations around inheritance. When beneficiaries are aware they will receive a significant inheritance, they sometimes maneuver to ensure they're seen in a favorable light by their benefactors.

In this chapter, we'll look at stories that reveal some pitfalls around death and money. Perhaps they will remind you of experiences within your own family. They might help you think about conversations with parents, siblings, or kids that will help you avoid creating similar situations. We'll see in Rhonda's story how inheritance brought out the worst in her siblings.

››› *Rhonda*

Rhonda, one of four adult children, lived in the same town as her mother all her life, while her siblings moved to other states. When their mother became terminally ill, Rhonda—a nurse—was the obvious choice to care for their mother, even though she had a family of her own with three young children. Rhonda and her mother enjoyed each other's company, and she was happy to help her through end-of-life transitions. Her siblings rarely came to town, even when Rhonda asked them to give her a break from the stress of constant caregiving.

When their mother died, Rhonda described her siblings as "swooping in like vultures." Her mother had promised her car to Rhonda, but one of her sisters wanted it for her teenage son, saying Rhonda had coerced their mother to give it to her. To avoid conflict, Rhonda let her sister have it. As they emptied the house and item after item was spoken for, Rhonda noticed that whenever she showed interest in something, one of her siblings wanted it. A heavily used wooden cutting board was one of the last items to be distributed. Rhonda had fond childhood memories of watching their father use the cutting board, chopping vegetables while her mom cooked. When nobody wanted it, Rhonda left with the treasured item that brought her great joy. She told me that if she'd let her siblings know she wanted it, one of them would have wanted it too.

Making decisions around death is fraught with emotion, especially when it comes to creating wills and trusts. I'm often involved in gathering financial information for clients to provide their attorney as part of finalizing their estate plans. Rarely does my involvement end with collecting information, as clients discuss emotional issues as they contemplate putting long-term decisions in writing. Consequently, I've been drawn into conversations that go beyond gathering documents and into the financial components of how assets will be divided among beneficiaries.

As we talk about what clients want to happen after their death, conversations can become emotional, more so when considering the special needs of a particular family member. Children's ages can become an issue as parents contemplate how knowing of their inheritance could impact them. Some kids aren't old enough for parents to know "how they will turn out," which makes parents wary of providing large sums for them to have at their disposal. Therefore, they often stairstep their children's ability to access their inheritance, allowing them to access specific amounts at certain ages, hoping wisdom will come with maturity. Since we can't control our kids from the grave (or anything else, for that matter), attorneys recommend safeguards for their protection. But without having a crystal ball to see their kids' futures, parents don't know whether these safeguards are helpful, or if they will handcuff their kids. I've observed that it's not unusual for parents to follow their hearts more than their attorney's advice, sometimes to their children's detriment.

››› *Frankie*

Having known three generations of Frankie's family, I never understood why her parents didn't put her inheritance in a trust. Even though she struggled with substance abuse from the time she was a teenager, she was clean and sober by the time her parents died. Still, they knew she had a shopping addiction that had replaced her earlier ones. I wonder if they wanted to demonstrate trust that Frankie would be able to handle financial affairs if given one last chance.

When Frankie's spending significantly diminished her initial inheritance within a few years, I asked what she would do when the money was gone. I was disturbed when she stated, matter-of-factly, "I'll kill myself." Frankie's parents would not have wanted her inheritance to lead to that. As her siblings watched how she spent the first money she inherited, they made legal provisions to keep her from doing the same with the remainder. Fortunately their intervention will likely mean that she'll have enough money to take care of herself, regardless of how long she lives.

››› *Jim and Lois*

As I worked closely with Jim, whom you met earlier in Chapter Six, he shared with me his concerns that Lois might be "overly generous" to her favorite charities if he died first. After he died, she wrote down the names of additional charity beneficiaries she wanted to add to her trust, but she didn't legally have it amended. Therefore, the executor could not make distributions beyond those listed in their joint trust. As Jim had handled their finances, Lois had been reluctant to state her wishes, thinking Jim would dismiss her preferences, as he'd done throughout their marriage. She could have amended her trust after he died, but because she didn't understand the legal requirements, the executor could not act on her handwritten instructions.

››› *Lucy*

As young adults, most of us don't have enough assets to need a will, but that doesn't preclude us from wanting to leave something of ourselves for others. I worked with a young client as she prepared to leave for college who has more financial assets than most kids her age, as her grandmother has been giving her annual gifts to reduce estate taxes for many years. Before leaving for school, she signed health care directives in both her home state and that of her university, as well as a Financial Durable Power of Attorney. She identified friends and charitable organizations to receive some of her money in the event of her death. She's been advised that she doesn't need a will at this time, as her assets are held in joint tenancy with her mother or in trust. She's to be commended for starting her financial life thinking ahead about these important issues and providing guidance to her parents in the unlikely event of her untimely death. Most young adults assume they will have a long lifetime ahead of them with plenty of time to make decisions. As time goes by, a common trajectory is that they have a family and accumulate significant possessions. It's typically at this point that people start to think about the importance of creating a will and/or trust, depending on the assets involved.

I recommend working with an estate attorney to guide you and your kids in making decisions like Lucy's. If you think you don't need an attorney, you can use legal templates from the internet that will provide guidance to whomever deals with your life matters, especially in the event of an unexpected death. As we saw in the story of Gail and Tom (in Chapter Six), who died in his thirties, death can happen—even while teaching a fitness class.

It's not uncommon for people to avoid making a will or to get bogged down in the process, never completing the questionnaire from their estate attorney. Countless considerations about what we "should" do with our money—such as fairness to all children, the specific needs of each child, their personalities, and our perception of their "best interest"—can become overwhelming. Attorneys who don't know our families well, if at all, may consider the legal issues but ignore the many psychological and emotional issues that get stirred up around death and dying. Additionally, it can seem like attorneys begin with an assumption that it's not wise to trust that our beneficiaries will "do what's right" after we're gone. Therefore, they tend to focus on the many possible legal pitfalls that may or may not happen.

The single most difficult issue I've observed that stops people from creating a will or trust relates to the care of their young children. Time and again, I've noticed clients who meet with an estate attorney and ask me to gather financial information to complete their questionnaire. When they have to name someone to care for their minor children, the process goes no further. A common roadblock happens when one parent wants the children to live with their parents or a sibling, while the other parent doesn't consider that person suitable to raise their children. Additionally, they worry about how their other family members might interpret not being chosen as the designated caregiver.

Rather than discuss the issue with their spouse around naming a person or couple, or why they don't want their children to live with a certain family member, they become emotionally frozen, stopping the process altogether. By stalling, they make an unconscious decision to wait, hoping they'll live until the children are no longer minors and they don't have to decide. I'm reminded of a friend who raised her sister's baby and toddler after a car accident killed the children's father and left her sister in a permanent vegetative state for more than twenty years, before she eventually passed away. Unexpected deaths happen, and choosing who will care for your children, difficult as it might be, is better than leaving the decision for someone else to make.

Let's see how inheritance can impact families.

Jack and Mary

Jack's parents revised their estate plan when they were in their seventies, when they had decades of information about the stability of their grown children's families. At the time, their children's ages ranged from mid-forties to late fifties and fell into three categories: (1) three had long-term marriages of thirty years or more, each with two children, making a total of six grandchildren; (2) a son, also in a decades-long marriage, with no children; and (3) an unmarried daughter without children. Even though each of their married children had been with their spouses for decades and the families had been close throughout those long marriages, the parents named their children as sole beneficiaries, with equal shares of their estate given to each. In the event that a child predeceased them, that child's share of the inheritance would bypass the child's spouse and go directly to their children, or revert to the other siblings if their child had no children.

While I understand that long-term marriages sometimes fail, there was no evidence that this was a possibility in any of their children's marriages. Jack and his wife, Mary, discussed how his parents' decision would impact their immediate family in the event of Jack's premature death. He instructed their children to provide whatever money Mary needed if he died before his parents. Regardless of how his parents structured their estate plan, he considered his inheritance to be his and Mary's before their children were entitled to it. Fortunately, their children understood and agreed that their mother should benefit from Jack's inheritance, so it didn't create a problem—but it could have.

››› *Kevin and Lily*

The situation Jack's parents created for Kevin, their son without children, seemed especially unfair as his siblings considered what their parents had done. Because Kevin had no children, if he predeceased his parents, his inheritance would go to his siblings rather than to his wife, Lily. Kevin and Lily had lived next door to his parents for several years, checking on them daily and doing a myriad of tasks for them. Because the siblings appreciated the care and attention Kevin and Lily gave their parents, they were appalled that Lily would get nothing if Kevin died before their parents. As things turned out, the parents predeceased all their children, so neither of these scenarios happened.

While I understand why their estate attorney recommended that they keep family wealth within their bloodline, I doubt he considered how the plan might have evolved.

⟫⟫⟫ *My Grandparents*

My grandparents were financially comfortable, having built three family businesses from early in their marriage. However, Grandad knew nothing about their finances, as Grandma handled their money and did the accounting for their businesses. Soon after she died of a heart attack at the age of sixty, he discovered the extent of his wealth. He became concerned that his stepdaughters (my mother and aunt) and their children were spending time with him just to gain favor so we could get his money. Even though my grandparents had been married since before I was born, and my brother and I spent so much time living at their house that we each had our own bedrooms, the closeness we'd had my entire life didn't stop him from suddenly thinking I was spending time with him primarily to gain access to his money.

Even though my grandparents' wills had split everything equally among their four adult children, he changed his after she died, leaving his estate to his children and grandchildren, with the exception of $10 each to my mother and aunt. Mom never deposited that $10 check, which she said felt worse than getting nothing at all.

››› *David, Deborah, and Alice*

In yet another family, David died unexpectedly in his mid-forties, and his wife, Deborah, remained close with his mother, Alice, who referred to her as her daughter rather than daughter-in-law. Deborah and her daughters were included in David's family's holiday gatherings, just as they were when David was alive. Deborah raised their girls alone and never remarried, remaining close with all of David's family. When Alice died some thirty-five years after David, Deborah wasn't a beneficiary in Alice's substantial estate. She was pleased when David's share of the inheritance was given to their daughters, but she was disappointed not to be recognized. More than financial consideration, Deborah was hurt to find herself excluded as part of Alice's family.

Pain and conflict after a loved one's death stay with us for a long time. There's no opportunity to clear up misunderstandings or ask about intentions after someone is gone. This will be true when we die, as well. As hard as it is to think about death, and even harder to talk about it, we convey our love to family members by providing clear written guidance to whomever deals with our financial affairs after we're gone. Even more helpful, having potentially difficult conversations with the person we've named to execute our wishes gives us the opportunity to provide them with understanding of our reasoning.

I have seen several instances where the person named as successor trustee or executor was not asked whether they would serve in that capacity, only to find out after their loved one has died that the burden is theirs. Often, the person has no knowledge of the deceased person's financial affairs, the location of important documents, or passwords. As difficult as it can be, talking to your executor about these matters while you're alive has more desirable consequences than leaving things to be misunderstood and sorted out after you're gone.

As we've reviewed many ways things can unravel after death, as well as some that could have unraveled but didn't, I invite you to consider how these stories can help you think about the pitfalls you want to avoid.

Some Practical Matters

In administering more than a dozen wills and trusts, I've dealt with issues that arise from differing state laws, a lack of written instructions to guide me, conflicting directives (likely written at different times during the decedent's life), and confusion when beneficiaries read instructions with differing interpretations. Often, in these cases, the attorney who drafted the documents is either no longer practicing or doesn't have the information needed to clarify the decedent's intentions. Furthermore, I have seen the aftermath of decisions that were included in wills but not shared with family members. When this happens, in addition to dealing with emotions around the death of a loved one, beneficiaries are often surprised to learn how the will differs from their expectations.

Sometimes, we forget what we put in our will. When reviewing it, we may find that changes in our lives make our earlier choices obsolete. For example, we first wrote our wills when we had one young daughter. As the attorney asked us to identify beneficiaries we would want our assets to go to in the event of common demise or if all our family members predeceased us, we named personal friends who were important in our young married lives. Ten years later, when we revisited our wills, we were surprised to see whom we'd named, as they were friends we'd been out of touch with for a number of years. A lot can happen in ten years that changes how we think about our final wishes. For this reason, attorneys recommend reviewing wills and trusts every five years.

In addition to legal documents that direct bequests to beneficiaries, one of the best ways to show love for your family is by having an "Estate Workbook." A friend calls this her "God Forbid" binder. It includes information needed at the time of death, such as:

- Personal information: birth certificate, marriage/divorce documents, Social Security, driver's license, and passport
- Financial information: bank account names, numbers, and locations; major assets and liabilities;

and credit card and charge account details

- Medical contacts: names and phone numbers of all medical providers
- Advisor contacts: names, phone numbers, and emails for insurance agents, attorneys, investment advisors, CPAs, and preferred realtor
- Insurance information: property, health, life, and burial policy numbers and locations
- Pet details: related wishes, and vet's name and contact number
- Burial information: burial wishes, cemetery plots owned, preferred funeral home, and burial plan
- Online access details: login credentials, especially for phones, computers, and key accounts
- Notification requests: names and contact information of people/loved ones to be notified of your death

This list is not exhaustive, but having this information collected in a single place is one of the most loving things you can do for whomever handles your affairs when you're gone.

SOMETHING TO THINK ABOUT

- Do you have a will or trust? If so, where is the original kept? Is it current?
- Have you shared your wishes with people who need to know them and told them where your documents are kept?
- Do you know the wishes of your parents, siblings, and adult children regarding their own deaths?
- Have your family members discussed whether they have named you as their executor or successor trustee?
- Have you discussed your wishes or estate plan with your children, if age appropriate?
- Do you know what your siblings would ask of you regarding their minor children in the event of their death? Would they want you to care for their children? If so, have they created documents to give you legal rights? Have they provided you with financial resources to care for their children?
- If you've named an executor or successor trustee, what does that person need to know about your affairs that you have not provided? Do they know they've been named? Do other family members know who you've named and understand why you chose that person (if you've chosen to tell them)?
- Have you set things in motion that might cause pain after your death that you can clarify now, while you're alive?
- If you don't have a will or trust, will you commit to creating one by a specified time?
- If you have an outdated will or trust, will you review it, revising it if needed, by a goal date?

PART IV:
Going Forward

As we head into the home stretch of this journey we're taking together, I'm hoping you've considered:

- the ways you think about money
- the consequences of that thinking, especially as they relate to important people in your life
- the sources of your beliefs, ideas, and habits
- conversations you've had—or are looking forward to having—with specific people about events that have shaped your relationship with money
- the habits you can change to alleviate negative feelings you have around money
- how you can develop a healthier, more constructive relationship with your money
- the possibility of achieving financial peace and well-being

Chapter 18

A Testimony: My Journey to Financial Wellness

I've had nightmares throughout my lifetime, with the same recurring theme. I'm in danger, with no avenue of escape. I was four or five years old when I had the first iteration of this dream. A man broke into our house, and I heard footsteps as he walked down the hallway and entered my bedroom. To avoid being seen, I hid under the bed. I could see his feet as he walked closer to the edge of the bed, and then he got down on his hands and knees to look underneath and discovered me there. My heart raced in terror as I saw his eyes looking at me. Since my twin bed was pushed against the wall, I was trapped with nowhere to go to get away from him. Typically, this is where I'd wake up, often crying.

Later in life, the danger in my dreams often found me on a tiny ledge of a high-rise building with nowhere to go. Again, a man was trying to grab me, this time through an open window in the building, and my choices were to jump to my demise or be caught. Sometimes, when I had this dream, I would wake Kent as I screamed for someone to help me.

I have no doubt these recurring dreams are tied to feeling backed into a corner with no way out—to fears about safety, security, and, later in life, specifically about money. When we were in the midst of the downward spiral of losing our business, our home, our lifestyle, and some of our friends, I desperately wished my grandmother were alive to save me as I had watched her save my mom by providing for us when Mom couldn't. The sense of hopelessness, despair, and yes, terror, from my recurring nightmares caused me to believe she was the only one who could help. I now know that belief kept me from being open to other solutions that eventually helped us move on from the seemingly endless losses.

I've shared much of my story around money throughout the pages of this book. Still, I'll leave you with some lifetime learning to provide evidence that change is possible:

- First and foremost, I share Warren Buffett's famous statement about his great luck at having been born in America.
- My second stroke of good luck came from having two sets of loving, helpful grandparents who stepped up to the plate to help our young mom provide loving support—both emotional and financial—for my brother and me.
- With therapy and self-help work, I have learned to appreciate the difficulties Mom faced, being too young and ill-equipped to care for herself, let alone two children. For a long while, I was angry with her for not providing the nurturing that we needed; fortunately, I've replaced those feelings with loving appreciation for her doing the best she could.
- I know the benefit of letting go of what doesn't matter. "Not my circus; not my monkeys" has

become my mantra, and it guides my choices related to time and energy.

- Hardship isn't the worst thing that can happen. I'm grateful for life experiences that hurt deeply at the time; I now see how the good that happened afterwards couldn't have occurred without the painful experiences. As Ashima Sarin says, "Darkness is in the folds of light."
- When we were going through our bankruptcy, the statement, "They can't eat us," helped me survive experiences I thought would destroy me. As evidenced by being here on Kaua'i to write this book, I was right—they could neither eat nor destroy me.
- People matter. Love matters. Experiences matter. Relationships matter. Abundance matters. Knowing each other's hearts matters.
- Money is a tool that allows us to have choices—some greater, some lesser. It's not what matters most.
- Knowing the amount we spend and what we buy serves us well.
- We are not alone in our struggles around money. Being willing to discuss our fears and vulnerabilities with trusted others can lighten our journey and lead us to peace.
- We must each find our own path to a healthier, more constructive relationship with money. Exploring the topics and stories in this book can help you find your way.
- It's never too late to learn, grow, and change your thinking.
- If I could go from being a frightened child who believed there would never be enough to living on

Kaua'i, basking in an abundant life, then you can transform your relationship with money too.

My grandmother had the following message taped to the top of her desk. I memorized it long before I was old enough to understand its meaning:

> *The grinding that wears to nothing a lesser stone merely serves to give luster to a diamond.*

We are all multifaceted diamonds.

Chapter 19

Your Journey to Financial Wellness

I hope the stories and experiences in this book have helped you realize that you're not alone in your angst around money. With your newfound understanding of ways others struggle with money issues, I hope you're encouraged to be kinder and more loving with yourself as you take this inner journey toward financial wellness. Maybe you'll even be able to enjoy the power you now have in your relationship with your money.

And in the process, I hope you've become more comfortable talking with important people in your life about money. Perhaps you've had conversations with family members to learn their understanding of ancestral issues that might be at work in your own life. If not, I hope you'll seek opportunities to open these doors, so you can begin to resolve the issues that cause you distress or discomfort around money.

If you wrote a letter to your money as we started this journey, you might want to write another one now to compare how your feelings have changed. And if you didn't write one in the beginning, you might write one now to launch your new relationship with your money, recognizing the power you have within you to create.

We've covered a lot of ground in these stories, some of which you may relate to and others that might not seem relevant to your life at this time. I hope you'll continue to recall them as you have new experiences with money and refer back to them often to use the lessons of others for your own benefit.

In thinking about your memories related to money, I encourage you to test your assumptions and be open to changing your perceptions, especially if those memories cause you pain. You have the power to choose not to let that pain drive your future as you move toward peace with money.

Delving deeply into your own experiences and beliefs about money will provide you with a foundation to understand your feelings and behaviors. With this new understanding, you're better equipped to make changes that lead to a relationship with money that is more positive and peaceful—and less stressful.

As I've said throughout this book, please be gentle with yourself and have compassion for those who have hurt you along the way. Put your arm around the child sitting on the curb and ask her to tell you about what's making her cry. Having a healthier, more constructive relationship with your money is new territory that needs patient kindness to evolve. You didn't develop the angst overnight that caused you to buy this book, and you won't overcome it overnight either. But I promise that you *can* have the financial life you want by taking one step at a time on this road toward making changes that will lead to a powerful, peaceful relationship with money. This path can calm your anxiety, build your confidence, create a friendly relationship that allows you to take control of your money, and prevent you from passing your struggles with money to your children.

I'd love to hear from you as you walk the remainder of your journey. You can reach me at tari@tarikvickeryauthor.com.

Namaste.

Notes

Chapter 1

1. Ashima Sarin, *108 Blessings: Alchemy for the Mind, Body and Soul* (CreateSpace Independent Publishing Platform, 2017), 184.
2. Sarin, *108 Blessings*, 76.

Chapter 3

1. Kristin Wong, "We're All Afraid to Talk About Money. Here's How to Break the Taboo," *New York Times*, August 28, 2018, www.nytimes.com/2018/08/28/smarter-living/how-to-talk-about-money.html.
2. Shmoop Editorial Team, "Money: The Economic Definition," Shmoop, last modified November 11, 2008, www.shmoop.com/study-guides/money-banking/economic-definition.html.

Chapter 5

1. Isadore Barmash, "RCA's Biggest Shareholder," *New York Times*, April 18, 1971, www.nytimes.com/1971/04/18/archives/

rcas-biggest-shareholder-seretean-developed-and-sold-coronet.html.

2. Robert Reinhold, "Desperation Descends on Oklahoma," *New York Times*, May 11, 1986, www.nytimes.com/1986/05/11/business/desperation-descends-on-oklahoma.html.

Chapter 8

1. Care.com editors, "Here's How Much Longer Women Have to Work to Earn the Same as Men," Care.com, last modified May 19, 2021, www.care.com/c/equal-pay-day-gender-pay-gap-by-profession.
2. David Swindle, "Pew: Wives Earn More Than or the Same as Husbands in 45% of Marriages," JNS, www.jns.org/pew-wives-earn-more-than-or-the-same-as-husbands-in-45-of-marriages.
3. The Bronfenbrenner Center for Translational Research, "Do Girls Perform Better in School?" *Psychology Today*, August 23, 2018, www.psychologytoday.com/us/blog/evidence-based-living/201808/do-girls-perform-better-in-school.
4. David Wessel, "Men Not at Work," Brookings, October 6, 2016, www.brookings.edu/articles/men-not-at-work.

Chapter 9

1. Chase Jarvis, *Creative Calling* (Harper Business, 2019), 55.
2. Samantha Subin, "Millennials, Gen Z Are Job-Hopping, but Contrary to Popular Belief, Maybe Not Enough," CNBC, February 28, 2021, www.

cnbc.com/2021/02/28/millennials-gen-z-are-job-hopping-but-maybe-not-enough.html.

3. Bureau of Labor Statistics, "Number of Jobs Held, Labor Market Activity, and Earnings Growth Among the Youngest Baby Boomers: Results from a Longitudinal Survey," U.S. Department of Labor, March 31, 2015, https://www.bls.gov/news.release/archives/nlsoy_03312015.pdf
4. Elle Luna and Susie Herrick, *Your Story Is Your Power: Free Your Feminine Voice* (Workman Publishing, 2018), 54.
5. Sally Schneider, "Phillip Glass: Renowned Composer, Taxi Driver, Plumber (with Music)," Improvised Life, June 11, 2014, https://improvisedlife.com/2014/06/11/phillip-glass-world-renowned-composer-taxi-driver-plumber.
6. CFPB Office for Older Americans and Office of Students and Young Consumers, "Social Security Offsets and Defaulted Student Loans," Consumer Financial Protection Bureau, last modified January 8, 2025, www.consumerfinance.gov/data-research/research-reports/issue-spotlight-social-security-offsets-and-defaulted-student-loans.
7. Sarah O'Brien, "Here's When Unpaid Debt Can Reduce Your Social Security Payments," CNBC, August 15, 2019, www.cnbc.com/2019/08/15/heres-when-unpaid-debt-can-reduce-your-social-security-payments.html.
8. Justin Bariso, "Google Has a Plan to Disrupt the College Degree," Inc.com, August 19, 2020, www.inc.com/justin-bariso/google-plan-disrupt-college-degree-university-higher-education certificate project-management-data-analyst.html.

9. The Education Plan, "With Vocational and Trade School Enrollments on the Rise, The Education Plan® Offers Savings Opportunities and Flexibility," Yahoo! Finance, October 20, 2021, https://finance.yahoo.com/news/vocational-trade-school-enrollments-rise-204500448.html.
10. Sreekar Jasthi, "The Most Educated Places in America," NerdWallet, August 3, 2015, https://web.archive.org/web/20220127051044/https://www.nerdwallet.com/blog/studies/most-educated-top-cities-2015.
11. Ishika Chawla, "CDC Releases Preliminary Findings on Palo Alto Suicide Clusters," *The Stanford Daily*, July 21, 2016, https://stanforddaily.com/2016/07/21/cdc-releases-preliminary-findings-on-palo-alto-suicide-clusters.
12. Yanan Wang, "CDC Investigates Why So Many Students in Wealthy Palo Alto, Calif., Commit Suicide," *Washington Post*, February 16, 2016, www.washingtonpost.com/news/morning-mix/wp/2016/02/16/cdc-investigates-why-so-many-high-school-students-in-wealthy-palo-alto-have-committed-suicide.

Chapter 10

1. Epicurus, "Gnomologium Vaticanum Epicureum (Epicurus Proposal)," in *Gnomologium Vaticanum*, ed. Leo Sternbach (Berlin: Walter de Gruyter, 1963).

Chapter 15

1. Life and leadership coach Julie M. Daley first introduced me to the term "Voice of Judgment"

(VOJ), which refers to our self-talk that often echoes our parents or other authority figures from childhood.

2. The Story of Stuff Project, "How Advertising Rewires Kids' Brains," Story of Stuff, April 25, 2019, www.storyofstuff.org/movies/the-good-stuff/how-advertising-rewires-kids-brains; American Psychological Association, *Report of the APA Task Force on Advertising and Children* (APA, 2004), www.apa.org/pubs/reports/advertising-children.
3. Common Sense Media for Families, "Junk Food Ads and Kids," posted October 11, 2013, YouTube, 2 min., 22 sec., www.youtube.com/watch?v=5ahMQwxN9Js.

Chapter 16

1. Abha Bhattarai, "The Average Millennial Has a Net Worth of $8,000. That's Far Less Than Previous Generations," *Washington Post*, May 31, 2019, www.washingtonpost.com/business/2019/05/31/millennials-have-an-average-net-worth-thats-significantly-less-than-previous-generations.
2. Kristen Bialik and Richard Fry, "Millennial Life: How Young Adulthood Today Compares with Prior Generations," Pew Research Center, February 14, 2019, www.pewresearch.org/social-trends/2019/02/14/millennial-life-how-young-adulthood-today-compares-with-prior-generations-2.

Acknowledgments

Coming to Kaua'i to write this book has enhanced my life in ways beyond my wildest dreams. The island nourishes my soul, supports me, and sustains me. I am grateful for being welcomed and held by its energy. In following Ralph Waldo Emerson's wisdom, "Once you make a decision, the universe conspires to make it happen," I could not have imagined how my journey would start as a decision to write a book and the universe would conspire to provide the life I love.

To my true believers: Thank you to all who said, "You should write a book," for encouraging my dream, believing in me, and holding me in your loving spirit.

To my clients, family, and friends whose stories fill these pages: Thank you for trusting me with your emotions, your journeys, and often, your children and elderly parents. Thank you for your courage and vulnerability as you shared the tender places where your emotions and money converge. Your encouragement continues to support me throughout my journey. Thank you for walking this path with me. I am honored and grateful to have a seat at your table.

To my team at Life Matters Financial Group: Thank you for years of rowing the boat, caring for the needs of our clients, and doing the heavy lifting to provide me with time to think and write.

To my publishing angels: Thank you for sharing your wisdom, guidance, and compassion for this debut author who had so much to learn from you. And thank you for making the book better.

And to the readers holding this book: Thank you for opening this window into some of your darkest places with hope of making peace with your finances and experiencing financial wellness. I am honored that you trust me to light your path.

About the Author

Tari K. Vickery is an author, Stanford-trained sociologist, entrepreneur, and financial wellness coach. With roots in a three-generation family of small-business owners, she helped build the operational foundations of several early-stage companies in Silicon Valley before founding Life Matters Financial Group, where for more than twenty-five years, she has managed the financial lives of individuals and families. Tari lives in Princeville, on the Hawaiian island of Kaua'i, where she continues to serve clients and write, drawing inspiration from the island's natural beauty.

Tari enjoys hearing from readers. If this book sparked reflection, questions, or conversation, you're invited to connect with her at tari@tarikvickeryauthor.com or visit her websites at www.tarikvickeryauthor.com and www.lifemattersfinancialgroup.com.

Author photo © Rachel Crane Photography

Looking for your next great read?

We can help!

Visit www.shewritespress.com/next-read
or scan the QR code below for a list
of our recommended titles.

She Writes Press is an award-winning
independent publishing company founded to
serve women writers everywhere.